How to coach
RUGBY FOOTBALL

How to coach
RUGBY FOOTBALL

Alan Black

WILLOW BOOKS

Willow Books
William Collins Sons & Co Ltd
London • Glasgow • Sydney • Auckland
Toronto • Johannesburg

First published 1990

A CIP catalogue record for this book is available from the British Library.   .

ISBN 0 00 218325 0 (paperback)
ISBN 0 00 218374 9 (hardback)

Commissioning Editor: Michael Doggart
Senior Editor: Lynne Gregory
Designer: Peter Laws
Illustrator: Craig Austin

This book was designed and produced by
Amanuensis Books Ltd
12 Station Road
Didcot
Oxfordshire
OX11 7LL

Printed in China

The pronoun 'he' has been used throughout and should be
interpreted as applying equally to men and women as appropriate.
It is important in sport, as elsewhere, that women and men should
have equal status and opportunities.

CONTENTS

THE AUTHOR

Alan Black was born in Gosforth, Northumberland and educated at Gosforth Grammar School. He studied Physical Education at Alsager College of Education (Certificate of Education) and Borough Road College (Bachelor of Education), followed by a Master of Science in Health Education at Chelsea College, University of London. He was Head of Physical Education in charge of rugby at Sir William Borlase's School, Marlow from 1971 to 1985.

As a club rugby player, the author played as lock forward/No.8 for Gosforth (1961-67) and Wasps (1968-78) where he was captain for three seasons. He also played county rugby for Northumberland and Buckinghamshire, and represented the Southern Counties versus Australia and Canada.

He gained the Rugby Football Union Coaching Award in 1977 and coached Wasps F.C. (1978-85), Middlesex County R.F.U (1982-85) winning the County Championship in 1985, and London Division (1982-85) which included matches against New Zealand (1983) and Australia (1984). He was Assistant Manager/Coach to England Under-23 XV on their tour to Spain in 1984, R.F.U. Senior Coach 1981 and R.F.U. Staff Coach 1984.

Alan was appointed Rugby Football Union Divisional Technical Administrator for London and South East Division in 1985, a post he currently holds. He is responsible for the development of the game throughout South East England; working on player development programmes with rugby players at all levels from Mini Rugby and New Image Rugby teams to Divisional and International players; also working on coach development courses with club coaches, school teachers and Sport/Youth Development Officers ranging from 'starter' courses, through preliminary award courses, to national elite courses.

In his work as a coach he has visited France, Canada, the U.S.A., Hong Kong, Spain, Singapore, Kenya and Holland. He has directed coaching courses for Thailand R.F.U. (1984); attended 4th Asian-Pacific Congress in Vancouver, B.C. (1983); World Cup in Australia and New Zealand (1987) and World Cup Technical Congress in Brisbane (1987).

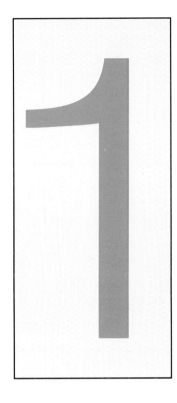

AN INTRODUCTION TO THE GAME

An Introduction to the Game

The game of Rugby Football began during a soccer match at Rugby School in 1823 when William Webb Ellis, a schoolboy, picked up the ball and ran with it. From that point onwards, Rugby Football was meant to be a running and handling game. Spectacular, exciting, International Rugby Union matches feature sustained periods of running and handling skills executed at speed in a competitive, contact situation. These skills are fundamental to successful Rugby Football, and their coaching forms the basis of this book.

Modern Rugby Football requires that all players, irrespective of their position, perform handling and continuity skills under pressure on an equal basis. Specialist requirements of players in the scrum and line out are needed, of course, but after these set pieces are played, there a no positions, no numbers on the players' backs, and everyone must be able to handle, run and support. This philosophy must be coached to players at the youngest age possible. The years between seven and twelve are often described as the golden years of skill acquisition. Handling, running, support and continuity skills should be acquired at an early age and the coach must emphasize the direction of his coaching towards this end.

Child development studies underline the fact that when it comes to skill acquisition, coaches must remember that children are children and not 'mini adults'. Make use of Mini Rugby, for example. This is a form of the game designed for juniors which reduces the number of players from 30 to 18, plus the referee. Yet even this may be too demanding for children at first. Playing four-a-side is described in the Rugby Football Union (RFU) publication *Even Better Rugby* and has the great advantage that it presents the basic structure of the game with an absolute minimum of players, so children do not have to deal with extra bodies who probably don't know what they are doing. Similarly playing four- and five-a-side helps get away from the 'beehive' games that children play where only a few actually succeed, and it encourages the development of skills. Smaller groups also reduce the number of options that different situations present which helps guide children in the making of decisions. Before eight years of age, few children play easily in large groups and team work is difficult, if not impossible. It pays to keep groups small and not to force children into situations which are beyond their capabilities. Mini Rugby provides a smaller pitch as well as fewer players which makes it easier for children to deal with both the physical and pyschological demands of the game.

It is easy to categorize children into positional profiles much too early in their careers. For example, Bill Beaumont was a full back at school before graduating via Fylde fourth XV to become an outstanding lock forward and captain of England and the Lions. Gareth Edwards, meanwhile, was an outstanding athlete and soccer player before specializing in Rugby Union Football and becoming one of the outstanding scrum halves of all time. Therefore, early specialization in a position is not recommended; focus upon the acquisition of general and basic skills. Premature emphasis upon playing position may also inhibit an understanding of the way the total game is played. It is preferable for all players to have a general understanding of the game before specific positional requirements are introduced.

In New Zealand where Rugby Union Football is a way of life, if not a religion, and where children play and observe the game as a high profile sport, most young players will arrive for their first rugby lesson in a club knowing and probably understanding the rudiments of the game. In most areas of Britain, however, this is not the case, and apart from watching snippets of the five nations championship, other International matches and 'Rugby Special' on TV, players will arrive with very little idea of the laws, tactics or skills involved in the game. From the first day that players arrive for a rugby coaching session be it at school, a club, sports centre or park, the most important elements to stress are that Rugby Football is about fun and enjoyment. Beginners

AN INTRODUCTION TO THE GAME

INTRODUCING RUGBY, A COACHING CONTINUUM FOR NON-CONTACT, NEW IMAGE RUGBY

1. ANY SHAPE AND SIZE, BOYS AND GIRLS CAN PLAY. ADULTS CAN PLAY TOO.

2. ANY NUMBERS PER SIDE. KEEP NUMBERS SMALL. REMEMBER HUNDREDS OF PASSES = SKILL ACQUISITION OPPORTUNITIES. SEE BELOW FOR SUGGESTED TEAM DEVELOPMENT.

3. SKILL PREVAILS. TACKLE = TWO-HANDED TOUCH.

4. GRADUALLY INTRODUCE THE CONCEPT OF SCRUM/LINE OUT BUT EMPHASIZE CONTINUITY.

5. PLAY ON ANY SURFACE. VARY THE SIZE OF THE PITCH.

AGE SEVEN	AGE EIGHT	AGE NINE	AGE TEN	AGE ELEVEN	AGE TWELVE	AGE THIRTEEN
Small numbers. Pass any direction. Two-handed 'touch' tackle.	Small numbers. Pass backwards. Passive scrum. 3 Forwards. Nearest players go into scrum. Free pass restarts.	3 Forwards. 6 Backs. Passive scrum. Free pass restarts. No kicking. Scrum half restricted - stays behind scrum until ball cleared.	3 Forwards. 6 Backs. Passive scrum. Passive line out. 2 jumpers. 1 thrower, see 'Laws'. Free pass restart. No kicking. Scrum half restricted.		5 Forwards. 7 Backs. Same 'Laws' as 10 and 11 but introduce tap penalties.	

THESE SUGGESTIONS ARE GUIDELINES ONLY

BE FLEXIBLE AND ADAPT THE 'LAWS', NUMBERS AND PITCH SIZES TO SUIT YOUR CIRCUMSTANCES.

should play some form of the game from the very first lesson. Participation in small-sided games in restricted areas, where players are free to pass in any direction and where tackling is eliminated, should form the initial introductory phase of the game. Thereafter progress them along a carefully structured 'Introducing Rugby' continuum as illustrated in the diagram opposite on page 10.

Beginners must have an understanding of the laws or rules of the small-sided game they are playing and, equally, of the correct spirit in which the game should be played. This applies from the first three- or four-a-side small game play to the full fifteen-a-side game.

Rugby Football is a relatively complex game in that the objective is to make forward progress while passing the ball backwards, and players need to possess a wide range of skills, a high level of fitness and a full understanding of the game if they are to be successful in the modern adult game. Careful, planned and structured coaching for beginners is essential if their basic skill levels are to established in the early years.

PLAY
PASSING • CATCHING
RUNNING • EVADING
SUPPORTING

SPEND MOST TIME ON
THIS PHASE

RUCK & MAUL
SIMPLE ORGANIZATION TO
MAINTAIN CONTINUITY

SPEND LESS TIME ON THIS PHASE

SCRUM
LINE-OUT RESTARTS

SPEND LEAST TIME ON
THIS PHASE

The Villepreux model

A Model for Coaching Rugby to Beginners

Pierre Villepreux, one of the outstanding rugby coaches in French rugby and certainly one of its deepest thinkers, is an advocate of spectacular, open rugby. In his model for coaching rugby, illustrated in the diagram on the left, Villepreux would only coach handling, support and continuity skills to children between the ages of eight /nine to twelve/thirteen, before moving on to coach the more formal aspects of the game: the ruck and maul to start followed by the scrum and line out. Villepreux's view is that play between the set pieces is the most difficult aspect of play to coach, and unless young players are coached with this kind of emphasis they will become set-piece orientated. By learning all the necessary skills for play between the set pieces first, beginners gain an understanding of the flow of the game; an insight into 'total' rugby from a variety of playing positions which will improve their decision-making abilities.

Education

The eighties have seen significant and fundamental changes in the field of education in general and in the teaching of physical education and games in particular throughout Britain. Mixed physical education, health-related fitness programmes, games for understanding initiatives and the advent of the GCSE in physical education have been important developments in the area of physical education and games teaching. A major objective of the RFU, which has always had a close association with schools, has been to promote Rugby Football in schools and to assist with the moral, social, mental and physical development of pupils. The changing world of physical education games, sport and society has been recognized by the RFU and a number of educational initiatives are in progress to ensure the continued health and development of the game. For example, an RFU education pack is available for use by pupils and teachers in schools; video tapes and manuals produced by schools are available through Youth Liaison Officers for use in clubs; RFU teaching and coaching video tapes and publications are constantly updated and are recognized as models of good practice. New Image Rugby, a form of non-contact touch rugby that can be played by girls and boys on a variety of surfaces, is a recent development which has kept rugby football moving in line with educational changes towards mixed physical education. There are now some sixty Women's Rugby clubs in Britain and rugby is now truly a game for everyone in the family - mums and dads, girls and boys.

Rugby clubs have begun to reflect these educational changes and many clubs are now promoting New Image Rugby for boys and girls in addition to the established Mini Rugby programmes that exist chiefly for the benefit of boys. Local Authority recreation departments have also been enthused by New Image Rugby, and many authorities include New Image Rugby courses in their holiday sporting and play scheme programmes.

The Spirit of Rugby

The rules of the game of Rugby Union Football are known as Laws, but these Laws mean less to the game than a long-established, accepted spirit in which the game is played and supported. You will not find all the following in the Law book, but you find them in the hearts and minds of all true rugby players and supporters.

• The referee's decision is accepted without question on the field of play. After the game, let discussion begin over refreshments, perhaps with the referee! Remember, he not paid, and he serves the game for his own enjoyment.
• Retaliation plays no part in the game; restraint is a lesson well learnt and practised.
• From the touchline, we treat the opposition at times of success or tension as we would our own side. For example, we applaud (if a little less loudly) their good tries and are silent for their place kicker.

• Shouts from the touchline against the opposition or regarding any practice in contravention of the Laws should NOT be heard.
• Applause for the opposition and the referee after the game is warm and genuine; it takes two sides plus the referee to create an enjoyable game.

Summary

• Emphasize running, handling, support and evasion skills; emphasize play between the set pieces as in the Villepreux model.
• Teach ALL SKILLS to ALL PLAYERS; do not categorize children into specific positions too soon.
• Small group practices and small-sided games are appropriate when coaching beginners.
• Introduce rugby to beginners in gradual stages as suggested in the continuum.
• Be aware of changes in education and physical education; keep yourself up to date on sound teaching and coaching principles; take into account growth and the developmental stages of young players.
• The spirit of rugby involves fun and enjoyment - winning is only a part of this. Never shout at or ridicule a young player when a mistake is made or a game is lost.

COACHING RUGBY

Coaching Rugby

Coaching and Teaching

There is often confusion concerning the difference between teaching and coaching. Coaching begins after teaching has taken place and is aimed at helping individuals or groups of individuals in team and unit skills to produce a higher standard of performance. The essence of coaching is that it takes into account the ability, personality, age, and aptitude of the individual **before** the skill to draw the best out of the individual participant. Coaching progression will be achieved differently with different individuals, different groups, different units, different teams. There is no rigidity about coaching; a commonsense, flexible approach is necessary. Coaches must be able to adapt to the changing circumstances and actions of their players and the different environments in which they coach.

A coach must be able to coach and teach. Even at International level players are still learning, and whilst at this more senior level the coach will be chiefly concerned with organizing, motivating and polishing up already established skills, nevertheless some teaching is still involved.

Who is Going To Coach?

The educational changes discussed previously have meant that a wide variety of people are now involved as rugby coaches to young children and beginners. The schoolteacher will still be the coach in many situations whether he or she is a physical educationalist or a specialist from another area of the curriculum who helps with some games teaching. The enthusiastic mother or father or the dedicated club member who is anxious to plough back some of his earlier years enjoyment into the game are often the people who have become the new generation of coaches in rugby clubs throughout the world. Youth Development Officers employed jointly by national and local authorities and governing bodies of sport are on the increase. Likewise Sport Development

Officers and Sports Motivators employed in Local Authority recreation departments, busy at work in the community offering coaching services to educational establishments, sports centres, community centres and voluntary clubs and centres, will often also offer rugby coaching services.

The concept of the coach being a gnarled veteran of the rugby field is outdated, and increasingly coaches are to be found from all sectors of the community, all ages and both sexes.

The Role of the Coach

The following section concerning the role of the coach offers some suggestions as to the control and organization of beginners, as well as the planning and preparation of coaching sessions.

Do not try to absorb them all at once; work on a couple at a time and eventually they will all become second nature.

The coach is:
• a leader
• an organizer
• a manager
• a friend
• a counsellor
• a teacher
• a motivator
• an innovator
• a hero
• a 'fall guy'
• a decision maker
• a communicator
• a role model.

The coach needs to have:
• KNOWLEDGE of the game
• PRACTICE TECHNIQUES that develop skills
• POSITIVE ATTITUDES towards the game.

The coach has three basic areas of responsibility:
1. Player fitness
2. Skills and development
3. Motivation through fun and enjoyment.

Be Prepared

Children are very perceptive and know when a coach is confused, under-prepared or nervous. Children may suffer a decline in enthusiasm for coaching sessions if the sessions are not carefully planned. Prepare your sessions in advance on paper; often it is a good idea to have alternative plans up your sleeve in case circumstances change unexpectedly - if double the numbers turn up or the weather changes.

A sample model session for complete beginners is detailed in the diagram opposite. The sample session is offered only as an outline guide because it is not wise to lay down any rigid programme. The coach has to be flexible and adapt to any changing circumstance.

Planning the Coaching Session

While there is clearly no one correct way to coach, it is important that the coach is aware that the basic aim is to improve the quality of the beginner's performance, so that he acquires skills and can enjoy the session. Some players will progress more quickly than others and these individual differences must be taken into account. Each coaching session should be regarded as one of a series and should therefore be related to previous and subsequent sessions.

The coaching session should have:
• An aim related to the overall theme.
• An introductory phase with a warm up and plenty of activity which should be fun.

BACKGROUND INFORMATION
AIM OF SESSION: Get to kno

	ACTIVITIE
INTRODUCTORY PHASE	2 per grid. Carry ball. Stretching
DEVELOPMENT PHASE	Shuttle grid with
GAME RELATED PHASE	Run any a-try. Whe back the mate.
CONCLUDING PHASE	Fun partne and withou

EQUIPMENT/MATERIALS

RUGGBY COACHING SESSION

Complete beginners. First session.
each other. Enjoyment. Ball in TWO hands.

DATE: 6.9.90
TIME: 10.30 - 11.30 AM

PRACTICES	MINUTES	TEACHING/ COACHING POINTS	ORGANIZATIONAL POINTS
void partner.	**10**	Ball in two hands. Use 5 metre grids.	One ball each
elays across artner.	**15**	**Give** the ball to your partner.	Take care - no contact with adjacent grids.
here. Score- ouched, give all to a team-	**20**	Ball in two hands. **Give** ball - no passing yet.	Play 2 v 2 and then 3 v 3 in 10- or 15-metre grid.
ctivities with all.	**15**	Work with different partners - get to know the whole group	

REQUIRED: 26 PLAYERS - 26 BALLS. 13 GRIDS. CONES. BIBS.
PUBLICATION/ INFORMATION SHEET TO TAKE HOME.
USE THE REAR OF THIS SHEET TO EVALUATE THIS SESSION AND TO PLAN FOR THE FUTURE.

19

• A development phase based on the theme which will probably involve reinforcement of previously learned skills and the introduction of new ones.
• Some form of game whether it be unopposed, semi-opposed or a conditioned game.
• A concluding activity incorporating revision of progress so far and a cooling down period.
• Notes on the equipment required and safety factors.

Evaluate the session afterwards and plan for the next session. Write some notes on the rear of the coaching session plan.

Be punctual

The coach should start and finish the session on time. Make the first activity a fun activity and then most of the children will respond by being punctual, ready to begin when you are. Parents in the club situation and fellow teachers in the school situation are also expected to finish on time. This is the one occasion when the coach is not required to be flexible.

Watch the weather

Weather conditions are a major factor when deciding what to do in coaching sessions. A warm day in September presents a totally different coaching situation to that of a cold, wet February day. It is essential that you select your activities with care - maximum activity for a short period in deepest winter, and a more leisurely approach in the early or late parts of the season or during the summer. Always protect young children from weather. Insist that they are well clothed against the cold or the wet and use both judgement and discretion when weather conditions are severe - a very cold or wet child quickly becomes a disinterested child. Always have a weather option up your sleeve, ideally this would be an indoor sports hall facility but many clubhouses can be utilized effectively by the imaginative coach. Have cold drinks available in hot weather and hot drinks when it's cold.

Demonstrations

Demonstrations are valuable aids to learning but they must be of the highest quality. If the coach does not feel confident demonstrating himself then it its better that he finds someone else - another coach, an older child, or even a senior player. The better the player the greater the impact his or her performance will have upon the group. Keep all explanations, instructions and demonstrations as brief and simple as possible. You do not have to explain the finer points of the game or even the practice to begin with. Rather give the children a very quick demonstration and let them have a go themselves for a few minutes while you watch their performance. You can then gradually add more information as they are working or while they are resting.

Children become bored if they practise the same activity for any length of time. A careful eye must be kept on this and as soon as it is sensed that boredom is creeping in, start a new activity.

Age, ability and aptitude

Young children enjoy playing simple games with a rugby ball, running around and handling the ball as much as possible. Therefore, a games-based approach often proves to be the best framework for the coaching session. During the first sessions young children do not want to look at a rugby ball held in the coach's hand and listen to a lengthy discourse upon the dimension of the field and the laws of the game. They want to feel the ball, to pass it and run after it. Skills are best learnt by doing and not listening and watching. To help maintain interest, each session should contain a new skill if possible. As soon as this skill has been practiced it should be put into a game-like situation.

Coaching sessions should be organized as a result of previous work and should be seen as part of a series. The coach may, for example, work on a series of six coaching sessions on handling skills before moving on to a series of coaching session skills on running.

Remember that children thrive on variety. The more ideas and practices a coach possesses, the more variety he can offer to the players in his care. The New Image Rugby (non contact) approach enables children of different ages, sizes and physiques to participate safely and happily together. When the time comes to introduce contact and, in particular, tackling skills, then much more care is needed in grouping children of the same age, ability, and size.

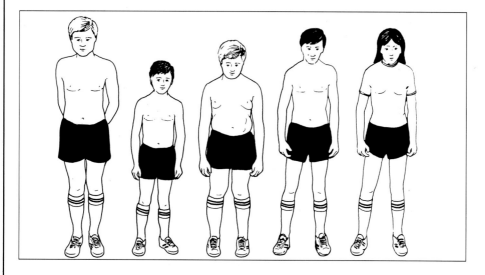

Individual differences
These players are the same age. Enjoyment and skill should be prime factors not physique.

Be specific

It is an easy mistake to try and achieve too much in any one session. Choose a limited, specific aim for your coaching session when preparing your session plan. The specific skill can then be taught, coached and developed into a conditioned game or free game situation. Your first activity will set the tone for the whole of your session. Try to make the first activity not only purposeful but also fun to play as this will grab and hold the enthusiasm of all the children. What you teach the group will largely depend upon their age and past experience. No matter what the content is, however, you must choose a practice which isolates the skill as much as possible. It is within this framework that coaching can take place with you, the coach, helping individuals with their performance.

The final part of your session is as important as the first. Once again it should be fun, but it should also include a game involving rugby skills that have been taught earlier in the season. Remember that the game is an ideal situation in which to emphasize your coaching points.

Evaluation

Try to evaluate your coaching session as you go along. Throughout the session try and make mental notes of what went well or what went badly and how you might improve your practices in the future. Get into the habit of making brief notes about the session so that your future preparation can benefit from this process. The sample coaching session plan emphasizes the need for constant evaluation by the coach.

Grouping

A large group of children should be divided into smaller units in order to keep the players working to capacity. This ensures that they are heavily involved in the activity which in turn leads to success and enjoyment. Remember that a child is more likely to acquire handling skill if he is receiving hundreds of touches of the ball during the coaching session. This will not happen in a large group situation when he may only touch the ball every five minutes.

For any coaching session involving handling skills, the ideal is to have one ball between two children. Let the children choose their own partner but encourage children to change partners fairly frequently. Encourage social interaction by getting children to work with new partners, encourage skilful performers to help their less able colleagues and where the coach is working with a mixed group of boys and girls, encourage them to interchange freely and work together.

Pairs can then join together to make groups of fours, sixes, eights and so on.

Key factors

'Catch the ball!'; 'Put the ball into space!'; 'Pass the ball!' - these expressions are all examples of the vague instructions sometimes shouted at groups of children playing complicated ball games. They give the performers some idea of **what** they should be trying to achieve but do little to explain **how** to achieve it. These instructions are not specific enough to give the performer the information to help him make a change. The coach must work to sharpen his ability to analyse technique. The diagram below puts this in the simplest terms.

Improving techniques in any sport follow a well- known pattern once the coach has decided which skill to coach. Briefly introduce the children to the skill in your practice. It is better to demonstrate the skill if you can then talk through it. As you demonstrate give the children some **key factors** or **action words** to remind them of the movements involved. These, for example, are for receiving a lateral pass: 'Watch the ball'; 'Reach towards the passer'; 'Hands at shoulder height, catch the ball early'.

Key factors for coaching the side tackle would be:
• Head behind the seat of the ball carrier
• Drive with the shoulder into the hip of the ball carrier
• Grasp both legs of the ball carrier below the knees
• Grasp tightly and hold on until the tackle is complete.

There are key factors for every skill in the game of Rugby and the coach must have them ready at his fingertips. When used well, key factors will remind the children of the required action during the execution of the skill.

The Rugby Football Union insures its qualified coaches while they are involved in coaching activities.

TECHNIQUE	PROBLEM	OBSERVATION	CORRECTION
CATCHING A PASS	DROPS MORE THAN ARE CAUGHT	CARRIES HANDS LOW. LOOKS AWAY FROM THE BALL.	"HOLD HANDS READY TO COLLECT PASS. WATCH THE BALL."

Be in control

The coach may be the most knowledgeable of people but unless he can control the group, much of that knowledge will be wasted or ignored. **All** children respond to a disciplined approach providing that it is not too powerful and overbearing. They must be made aware of what the coach expects of them, however, not only in the practice situation but also as visitors to other clubs and schools, and during the playing of other matches.The coach should be firm and positive but should always try to maintain an air of friendliness towards his charges. The children should enjoy the approach and method of the coach so that they will want to continue their participation. Having agreed to be a coach, certain responsibilities will have been accepted. Players' behaviour before, during and after training and matches is part of the package.

The coach must be active and continually move from player to player or from group to group correcting faults and giving plenty of encouragement and praise. Praise is one of the best motivators for young players. It may be a simple 'well done' or it may be to stop the group briefly and let them watch one of the children working and performing well. The children must be continually aware of the coach's presence because if young players sense that they are being watched then they are less likely to misbehave. Try to learn the names of all the players - the personal touch works wonders!

Try to coach from outside the coaching area (be this a grid, channel or area of the field), and only move into the centre of the area when you want to make a specific coaching point to an individual. This allows the coach an overall view of the players and the practice.

The control the coach exerts over the children is assisted by pre-planning and in particular by ensuring that all the equipment is ready for the smooth running of the coaching session. For example, rugby balls should be blown up and ready for use, ideally one ball should be available for every two children. Small, coloured, flexible grid markers are essential coaching aids to enable the rapid conversation of areas of the field into working and coaching areas in the form of grids, channels or small pitches. It is also extremely useful to have a stock of bibs available to identify different groups or teams.

Grids and the Grid System

The coaching grid is quite simply an area of the playing field which is sub-divided into series of squares (or rectangles). The grid size can be varied according to the size and age of the participants, the skill or activity being practised and the number of players involved. For very young players a five-metre square would suffice; for older boys and girls an eight-metre square may be appropriate, and squares of ten or twelve metres would be suitable for older boys or girls or club players.

Grids can be marked on a permanent or semi-permanent basis by the groundsman, but the disadvantage here is that the grid area can become unsuitable during periods of bad weather. By using small, coloured, flexible saucer-like cone markers grids can be marked on any section of suitable ground at a moment's notice.

Playground areas can be marked permanently (see illustration below) and groups can also be used on other artificial surfaces and in the sports hall. The rugby pitch itself is full of areas which may be used as coaching grids (opposite) but remember that there are areas more prone to wear during periods of fixture congestion or bad weather. Generally speaking, these are the areas between the 22- metre lines and the channel between the five-metre and the 15-metre lines along both touch lines. Choose the best area of ground which may quite often be the dead ball area because very little match play takes place here.

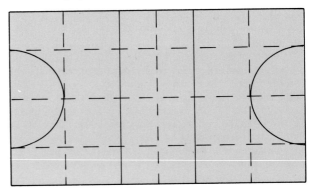

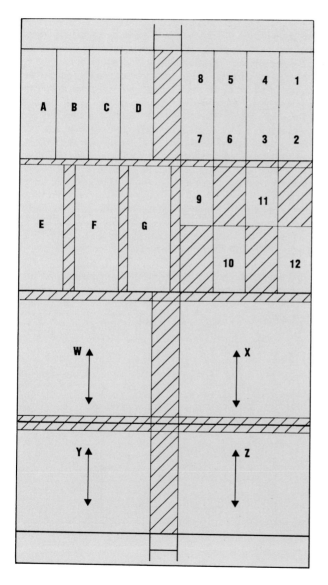

Grids and the grid system

Grids 1-8 (say 8m grids) and Grids A, B, C, D (say, 20m x 10m) are suitable for small group practices. Grids 9-12 and E, F, G are suitable for small-sided games . Never use 'common ' touch lines or goal lines because of the risk of accidental collisions. Set up 'buffer' zones between grids. Areas W, X, Y, Z can be used for five- to six-a-side games involving beginners. Always avoid goal posts even though they are padded. Areas W and X combined, Y and Z combined (or W and Y or X and Z) provide space for development through seven-, eight-, nine-, ten- and eleven-a-side games.

Channel work
Bottom left: Work along the channel, rest and work back again.
Bottom right: Work along channel A and return down channel B.

The advantages of using a coaching grid system are that it helps the organization of coaches and teachers, especially when confronted with large numbers of players, as it allows the pursuit of purposeful learning activities by a large number of players in a relatively small area. The coach or teacher can then control the activity of the group by sending them away to practise in their activity areas - the grids. Without this adaptation of specific space, chaos often results as units intermingle and the practice soon loses its effectiveness. This method of coaching allows a large number of players to be involved in enjoyable competitive activities in easily defined areas where the coach can see them, control them and make the necessary coaching points as he moves from grid to grid. Working with pairs or groups of three, four and five players in each grid ensures that every player has a great opportunity to handle the ball and become involved in the practice, thus sustaining his interest and developing skill. Skill practices can be developed by asking players in adjacent grids to play in small games against each other.

The need for constant variety in practices has already been stated and variety can be offered through the opposition, the size of the pitch and even by the constitution of the player's own team

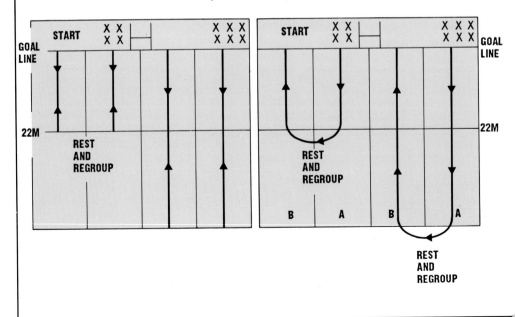

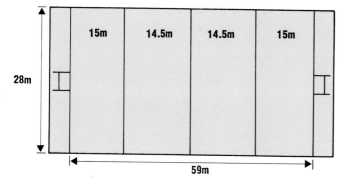

| 15m | 14.5m | 14.5m | 15m |

28m

59m

Suggested pitch areas for small-sided New Image Rugby and Mini Rugby games. Be flexible - alter the pitch size according to the numbers and age, aptitude and ability of the players.

being changed from time to time. The use of the grid can easily accommodate other practices, for example to practice effective, quick passing by a group, and a series of grids can be changed into a number of channels without the need to move cone markers. The illustration on page 27 shows how a channel system might work. Between four and eight channels could be fitted in across the width of an average rugby pitch. When coaching beginners and youngsters keep the channels fairly short in length, say 40 metres, to delay the onset of fatigue and to aid the control of the group by the coach. Groups can work in their own channel, or in one direction down channel A and in the reverse direction down channel B (see illustration opposite). Beginners should work to the 22-metre line or halfway line and back.

The use of grids and channels will be described throughout later chapters. The system is a valuable aid for all coaches from beginner level up to International standard. The illustrations above and on page 30 show how other areas of the rugby pitch can be adapted to cater for small game situations.

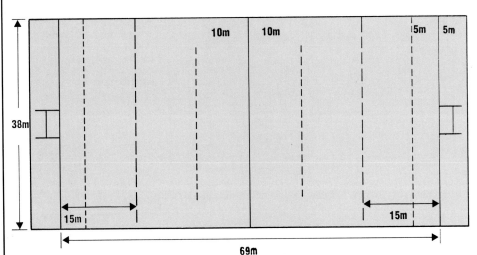

Suggested pitch areas for small-sided New Image Rugby and Mini Rugby. These are guidelines only.

The Skills Staircase

The skills staircase offers the coach a coaching progression and checklist. Proceed gradually up the staircase but always be prepared to return to the lower steps for correction and COACHING to take place.

Mental and Psychological Aspects

Remember that a child is not an adult! The implication of this statement is that the young rugby player should NOT be playing the same game as the adult player. In order to better meet the needs of the young player, the game should be modified taking into account:

1. Young players are unaccustomed to highly competitive environments.

2. Young players do not have, initially, a 'win at all costs' or 'pot hunting' approach.

3. Young players' levels of physical fitness vary greatly.

4. Young players see an improvement in personal performance and acceptance by their team-mates as worthwhile goals.

The game becomes an extension of the practice, an ongoing learning situation. The basis of success in coaching rugby to

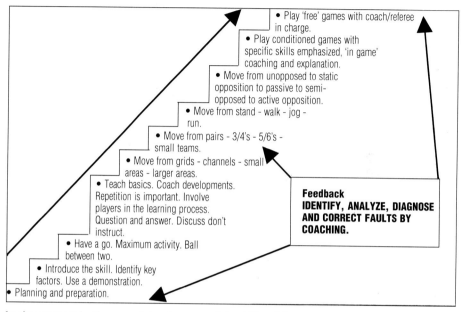

- Play 'free' games with coach/referee in charge.
- Play conditioned games with specific skills emphasized, 'in game' coaching and explanation.
- Move from unopposed to static opposition to passive to semi-opposed to active opposition.
- Move from stand - walk - jog - run.
- Move from pairs - 3/4's - 5/6's - small teams.
- Move from grids - channels - small areas - larger areas.
- Teach basics. Coach developments. Repetition is important. Involve players in the learning process. Question and answer. Discuss don't instruct.
- Have a go. Maximum activity. Ball between two.
- Introduce the skill. Identify key factors. Use a demonstration.
- Planning and preparation.

Feedback
IDENTIFY, ANALYZE, DIAGNOSE AND CORRECT FAULTS BY COACHING.

beginners must be the correct development of the skills of the game and not the full-time score of the game being played.

The Skills Staircase

Fitness

'Young children are naturally fit'. This often expressed opinion has been bought into question by modern research which indicates that many children spend up to six hours a day watching television. Many children have a sedentary way of life and it is wrong for the coach or teacher to assume that the young child is naturally fit. Children will not, however, be motivated to return to the rugby coaching arena if the coach or teacher turns out to be a 'lion trainer'! Fitness work needs to be enjoyable and as closely related to the game as possible such that the children are so heavily involved in the activity that they do not realize that any specific fitness work is going on. Fitness work can be made enjoyable by the judicious use of relays, shuttle runs, skill circuits and small-sided games.

There will be a fitness element in much of the work done by the well prepared coach. Much of this work will be skill orientated with a fitness component, but 'cold blooded' fitness work for young children is often a demotivating force.

The importance of the introductory activity in any coaching session has already been emphasized but this introductory activity should contain some warm-up work and in particular some stretching activities. Aerobic and anaerobic mechanisms can be developed during skill practices and during the actual playing of games or conditioned games. Strength can be improved by using partner activities such as arm rowing and piggy back carrying. Flexibility can be improved during the warm-up stretching; during pauses in activity and in the post activity period. Flexibility activities should proceed slowly and steadily with the aim of putting the muscles and joints through a full range of movement. Speed can be improved through participation in skill practices, executed quickly, and through relay and shuttle work activities. Running skills and evasive qualities can be developed through working with the ball in areas that are congested by other players.

In order to play New Image Rugby or Mini Rugby well, children have to be fit and, as fitness is a temporary phenomenon, it is the coach's on-going duty to ensure that the players in his charge are fit to perform the tasks asked of them, whether in the practice or the game situation. Physical conditioning programmes should be planned so that the player is fit enough to participate without becoming unduly fatigued.

As a general guideline:
• Under eight years - fun activities
• Eight to eleven years - light aerobic activities
• Twelve years on - a gradual increase in intensity taking into account **individual differences** and the need for **personal programmes.**

Young players have a very slow recovery rate. They will be unable to work intensively in short bursts with limited recovery time. They will however be capable of working for a considerable time at a low level of intensity. Practices should be SKILL intensive with a fitness element but not fitness intensive.

Weight training is not recommended for players under sixteen and then only under close supervision.

BACKGROUND INFORMATION AIM OF SESSION:	
	ACTIVITIES
INTRODUCTORY PHASE	
DEVELOPMENT PHASE	
GAME RELATED PHASE	
CONCLUDING PHASE	
EQUIPMENT/MATERIALS	

RUGBY COACHING SESSION   DATE:
                             TIME:

RACTICES	MINUTES	TEACHING/ COACHING POINTS	ORGANIZATIONAL POINTS

REQUIRED:

USE THE REAR OF THIS SHEET TO EVALUATE THIS SESSION AND TO PLAN FOR THE FUTURE.

Notes
1. Note previous progress and anticipate any new problems.
2. Note whether a new skill is being introduced or whether reinforcement will take place.

3. Keep explanations brief; use a demonstration; then have a go!
4. Have an idea of time allocations but BE FLEXIBLE and adapt to the circumstances.
5. Use **key factors** here.

6. Note numbers in groups, grids or channels in use, number of balls.
7. Ensure everything is available where and when you require it.

Summary

- A coach must be able to teach and coach.
- Coaches come from all sectors of the community, all ages and both sexes.
- Preparation and planning are essential.
- A coach must be in control and must be punctual.
- Use your voice effectively. Avoid unsavoury comments.
- Take into account individual differences in age, size and skill.
- Explain, demonstrate, then let players 'Have a go'.
- Use plenty of variety in your coaching. Beginners easily become bored.
- Do not try to cram too much into one session.
- Know the **key factors** of a skill.
- Evaluate your coaching sessions.
- Safety - be more careful than the most careful parent!
- The use of grids and channels will aid effective coaching.
- Do not accept that young children are naturally fit; they may be, but require regular bouts of vigorous physical activity to keep them so.
- Reward effort as well as achievement, enthuse and support all players.
- Fun, enjoyment, fitness and skill acquisition are the prime objectives of the Rugby Football coach.

HANDLING SKILLS

Handling Skills

Passing and Catching

These simple skills are fundamental, basic skills of Rugby Football and young players should have abundant opportunities to catch and pass the ball.

Beginners should work in pairs in a small grid (say five metres) with one ball between two players. The passer should pass the ball to the catcher and they should be only two/three metres apart. Begin with both players remaining static and gradually introduce walking, jogging and running. Gradually move the catcher to more than three metres away and vary the length, speed, direction, flight and trajectory of the pass. (Pass in any direction at this stage, see adjacent illustration).

The **aim** of the practice session is to pass over a few metres to the target area of the catcher who is stationary at first and later moves. The catcher should consistently catch the ball.

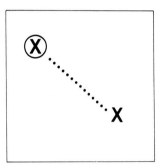

Ⓧ	player with ball
X	player(s) in support
☐	opponent
·········	path of player
- - - - -	path of ball

Passing - the key factors
1. Hold the ball in both hands, fingers spread down the seams.
2. With straight arms, swing across the body, pendulum fashion.
3. Look at catcher and aim for the target area.
4. Follow through with arms after the pass.
5. Keep feet comfortably apart, balanced.

Catching - the key factors
1. Watch the ball.
2. Reach towards the passer - set a 'target'.
3. Position hands at shoulder height.
4. Catch the ball early.
5. Hands, fingers and arms extend - 'meet and greet'.

Major faults
Passing
• Trying to pass too far
• Passing too hard

The target

• Spin passing (not always appropriate!)
• Not looking
• Not passing into the target area.

Catching

• Looking away from ball
• Carrying hands too low
• Poor arm extension
• Failing to 'meet and greet'.

Skill development

1. Still in two's in a five-metre grid continue to vary types of pass, distances and speeds

Continue to vary the movement of player. Progress from standing still, to walking, jogging and, finally, running.

2. Amalgamate pairs from adjacent five-metre grids to form ten-metre grids and work with four players

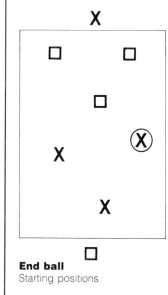

End ball
Starting positions

Pairs work with original partners on similar activities as above, but they now have to avoid contact or interference with the other pair in their grid who are involved in the same activity with their ball.

Key factors
• Avoid contact
• Find space
• Keep moving and keep looking.
 Also reinforce key factors regarding initial catching and passing exercises.

Further suggestions
As players become more skilful and confident move into groups of six, eight, ten or twelve using the same activities but allowing more space, say a 20-metre grid for groups of twelve.
 Again, once players can cope with this development, reduce the space available and set fresh challenges.

3. In groups of four work in a ten-metre grid, three versus one
The single player tries to intercept the ball being passed in any direction by the three. The three passers cannot run with the ball but must run off the ball into space.
 How many passes can the three make before the ball is intercepted? The single players cannot tackle or 'over-guard' the ball carrier. The emphasis is upon pass interception in flight. Change interceptor each time. Reinforce key factors.

4. Corner ball, three versus one practice in ten-metre grid
The single player tries to escape as the three attempt to tag him by touching him while in possession of the ball. No running with the ball is permitted; the players must run off the ball and put pressure on the single player. The ball must not be thrown 'at' the single player, he must be touched with the ball. Change the single player each time.
 Reinforce key factors.
Develop the practice to three versus two; three versus four etc.

5. End ball, four versus four practice in ten to 15-metre grid (see illustration).
Amalgamate two groups of four and play four versus four in 10 to 15-metre grid. In 'end ball' the players in possession cannot run

with the ball, they have to run off the ball. No tackling or 'over-guarding' is permitted. The aim is to inter-pass to get the ball to the team-mate in the end zone. Only good two-handed rugby passes are allowed. The outfield player who scores by passing to the player in the end zone takes his place as target player in the end zone for successive practices.

Key factors
Reinforce the key factors of catching and passing.

Further suggestions
Progress to playing six versus six, seven versus seven, eight versus eight, etc. in larger grids. If necessary have two or three players as targets in the end zone.

New Image Rugby

Using the grid sizes and group members as for end ball (activity 5), introduce the concept of the ball carrier being allowed to run with the ball and having to pass the ball when touched by an opponent.

The New Image 'tackle' or two-handed touch on the hips is illustrated overleaf. From the beginning insist on good technique - the tackler's head should be behind the ball carrier and he should touch both hips with two hands. From this starting point the contact, total tackle can be taught later.

When proceeding from end ball to New Image Rugby use a similar progression from partner work, through three versus one, six versus two activities as described earlier in this chapter.

Progression programme for New Image Rugby

1. Partners work in five-metre grid
The ball carrier moves around the grid attempting to avoid being 'tackled', New Image Rugby style, with a two handed touch, by his partner. The players have three 'lives' each, then they change roles.

New Image Rugby tackle

The tackler simultaneously places two hands on the hips of the ball carrier. The ball carrier passes immediately.

2. Three versus one practice in a ten-metre grid

One 'tackler' attempts to touch with both hands on the ball carrier's hips. The ball carrier must then pass the ball immediately to one of two colleagues. How many passes can the player make without a mistake? How many passes in one minute?

Further suggestions

Advance by playing six versus two, five versus three and four versus four.

3. Play three versus three, four versus four upwards, varying the size of the pitch accordingly

Play to New Image Rugby rules passing in any direction. The ball carriers' objective is to retain possession and score a try by touching down the ball over their opponents' goal or try line. The player touching down the ball must exert downward pressure and ideally a static ball should be touched down. The concept of the traditional rugby try 'touch down' is relevant on grass pitches but players may score by breaking the line while carrying the ball, American Football style, where the game is played outdoors on artificial surfaces or indoors in sports halls.

The tacklers can tackle (two-handed touch) the ball carriers who must pass the ball immediately. Possession is lost or regained either by an interception, a mistake where the ball goes loose and possession is gained by the non-offending side - the advantage law in its simplest and clearest state - or where a mistake or offence (in this case usually a ball carrier not passing the ball quickly enough when tackled) is noticed by the referee and a stoppage results.

In case of such a stoppage, the game is restarted with a **free pass restart** by the non-offending team. The player executing the free pass restart must pass the ball to restart play; he cannot run with the ball. Here we have the concept of the restart of play being introduced. The player executing the free pass restart must not be overguarded by the opposition; he must have a free area to be able to initiative play with a pass to a colleague, so defenders must retreat say five metres, see illustration.

Once play has been restarted, players can move freely in the grid. Restart play after a score by the team that has conceded the 'try', taking a free pass restart from the centre of the grid.

Development from three versus three and four versus four in small areas to seven versus seven or eight versus eight in larger areas.

However, do not allow the larger game to become the norm in your coaching session. Constantly change your approach and evaluate progress.

Constantly reinforce key factors in your coaching and reduce numbers to the minimum, take players back to the small grid situation for the correction of faults that will occur and for further teaching, coaching and skill development to be facilitated.

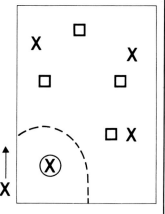

Free pass restart zone
New Image Rugby, four versus four in grid 15m x 25m. Player X taking the free pass restart is allowed a free zone. No opponents can close guard or over guard.

Passing Backwards

The next step in the gradual introduction to 'total' rugby is to teach the concept of passing backwards. Beginners will by now have learnt the basic handling skills of the game and will understand, to a greater or lesser extent, the flow of the game. They will also have learnt the concept of 'try' scoring and at this stage lots of tries should be scored during the small-sided games the beginners are playing.

To introduce the 'pass backwards' we have to go back to the small grid area in pairs. Begin by walking in pairs across the grid making one backward pass. Return across the grid with the other partner making the pass. Reinforce the key factors to this skill which are listed in the introductory section on handling skills.

Keep the pass short, say two metres at first, and once skill levels and confidence increase move on to long passes up to five/six metres.

Passing backwards

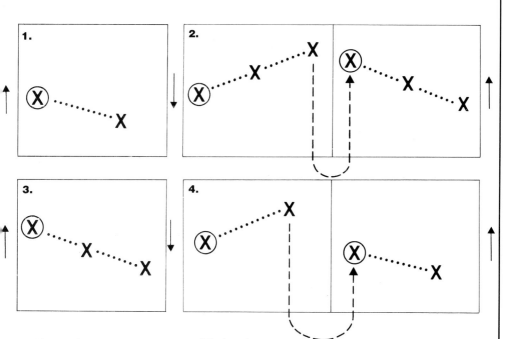

Using a five-metre grid (1) progressing to five-metre channels (2). Using an eight-metre grid (3) and progessing to eight-metre channels (4).

The key factor regarding the pendulum swing is even more important now that we are passing backwards. Gradually increase the pace from walking to jogging to running quickly.

Players should only make a single pass while they cross the grid. Keep it simple so that each partner has an idea of when he is in front with the ball or behind without the ball. The coach should say 'get in front when you have the ball' and 'stay behind when you don't have the ball'.

Now make the grid larger or move into channels and encourage the players to make consecutive passes while travelling across the grid or along the channel. The ball carrier must 'get ahead' or 'get out in front' if a backward pass is to be executed. The next progression involves working in a grid or channel area with three players where the middle player has to take and give a pass in the same movement or, with beginners, in as few strides as possible See illustrations above.

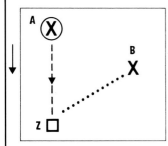

CORRECT
Player A runs straight to "fix" opponent Z and colleague B is free.

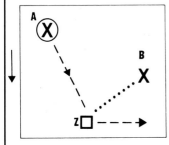

NOT CORRECT
Player A does not run straight and does not 'fix' opponent Z who can also now cover player B.

Progress by making more passes per player and more sequences of passes. Constantly change the middle player.

Move into fours so that there are now two middle players who have to catch and pass in one movement and two wing/end players who only receive or pass in one direction. Again change end and middle players.

Introducing Opposition

We have now introduced the concept of the pass backwards but have begun with unopposed practices. Now we move on to the gradual introduction of opposition.

Use three versus one in a grid of say ten metres. Begin by allowing all players to walk only. The defender can either make a New Image Rugby two-handed touch 'tackle' or try to intercept the ball. By running in a straight line to draw or commit or fix the defender, and by timing the pass correctly, the ball carrier can set his colleagues free to 'score'.

Progress from walking to jogging to running, still three versus one. Allow a slightly larger grid if space is the problem. Change the defender regularly and encourage the ball carriers to find solutions, to make decisions in the light of the situation and the reaction made by the defender. Considerable decision-making skills are required here and abundant decision-making opportunities must be made available to the ball carriers/attackers.

Key factors for the ball carriers
As for previous handling skills, but in addition:
• Look at the receiver when you are passing the ball, not at the defender. Look at the target area where you are aiming to pass the ball.
• Run straight to 'fix' the defender. Commit the defender and pass to set your colleague(s) free.
• Time the pass; not so late that the defender can intercept and not so early that the defender has time to turn his attention to your team-mate(s). See illustrations top left.

Lines of Running

Beginners must be encouraged from the earliest session to run straight, that is, parallel with the touchline or in the grid/channel situation parallel with the sideline.

The encouragement of the pass receiver to set a target will help because 'the hands out at shoulder length' and 'reach for the ball' key factors assist in keeping the receiver running straight. We will come back to more advanced line-straightening strategies later, but the concept must be laid down in these early, grid, channel and small-game situations. Do not allow the receiver to drift sidewards when taking the ball. He should rather move towards the passer and keep the lines of running straight.

From three versus one move on to four versus two, three versus two, five versus three, six versus three, six versus four and so on, gradually building up the level of opposition as the players become more skilful and confident.

Move on to playing small New Image Rugby games incorporating passing backwards and the two-handed touch tackle with three versus three, four versus four, five versus five and so on using a variety of pitch sizes to suit the participants. Restart play with a free pass restart when a mistake or an offence occurs and there is no advantage to the non-offending team. The ball carrier must pass the ball immediately after he has been touch tackled. 'Immediately' means as soon as possible with absolute beginners, as long as they are making an attempt to pass the ball. Where more experienced players are involved the pass must be immediately after the touch tackle. What must be avoided is the one-armed method of carrying the ball. If the ball carrier has the ball under one arm then he is obviously not in a position to pass the ball immediately. So avoid the one-armed carry - say no one-armed bandits! Key factor - carry the ball in two hands.

Once players have grasped the concepts of passing backwards, the two-handed touch tackle and understand the flow of the game it is time to introduce some of the other restart concepts of rugby i.e. the tap restart, the scrum and the line out. Again emphasize the need for gradual progression and refer to the two model continuums suggested for 'Introducing Rugby' to beginners.

The ball must be carried in two hands

Note
Remember the guidelines of flexibility and commonsense. For example, a school pupil playing games for four or five hours a week will plainly move more quickly along the continuum than a youngster in a club receiving ninety minutes coaching a week. Remember too individual differences.

The tap restart

The essence of New Image Rugby is to develop handling, running and support skills in youngsters and beginners. Therefore the free pass restart is the only restart phase introduced in the first and perhaps the second year of playing the game.

The tap restart is a step nearer to traditional rugby. Use the tap instead of the free pass restart when appropriate. The ball should be placed on the ground at the place of the offence: the 'tapper' taps the ball, picks it up and moves it to a team-mate. The 'tapper' must pass the ball, he cannot run off with it. The ball must be propelled through the mark at the point of the offence, and if the 'tap' is taken from the ball in the hand then the ball must be propelled again, in this case through the air.

The time when the tap restart is introduced is also the time to teach the pass off the ground or the scrum half pass, dive pass or pivot pass.

Picking up the Ball

Sometimes in the earliest stages of grid work, channel work, small-sided games and New Image Rugby it will be necessary for players to pick the ball up from the floor, the ball having arrived there usually because someone has dropped it. The ball may be static on the ground or it may be moving.

Static ball
Key Factors
1. Approach from the side
2. Place the rear foot close to the ball
3. Keep the eyes on the ball
4. Bend the knees
5. Secure the ball,with the rear hand sweeping the ball into the front hand.
6. With the ball in two hands, straighten the knees and drive away.

Rolling/moving ball
Same key factors as for the static ball but anticipate the point of pick up, time the approach, and accelerate in to the pick up area and drive away.

On some occasions it will be advisable, because of the pressure from the defence, for the player picking up the ball to remain in a strong position in order to pass to a colleague to maintain continuity.

Key Factors
• Keep a wide foot base ('wide is strong; narrow is weak')
• Straddle the ball
• Hold the ball at arms length in the fingers and pass the ball quickly away to a supporting player.

Falling on the ball
Where there is considerable pressure from the opposition and the moving or static ball on the ground has to be secured then it may be necessary to fall on the ball bodily to secure it properly. This

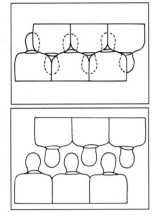

The binding of the scrum

is especially true in wet weather conditions. Choose the correct time to teach this skill - a wet day when beginners can confidently go to ground without the risk of injury. Do not teach this skill in hot, dry conditions where 'grass burns' and sore knees, elbows and hips can occur.

Key factors (moving or static ball)

• Keeping eyes on the ball, fall alongside it

• Keep the body between ball and opposition - back towards the opposition

• Secure the ball with two hands

• Get up immediately and move away or move the ball away as quickly as possible.

The Scrum

The tap restart is used to recommence play after an offence such as the ball carrier not passing the ball quickly enough following a two-handed touch tackle, a deliberate knock forward or a player kicking the ball. A scrum can be used to restart play after a forward pass or a knock on where no advantage is available to the non-offending team. The concept of the scrum is introduced in New Image Rugby but the team which puts the ball into the scrum has possession guaranteed. The opposition cannot push or wheel the scrum or strike for the ball. All players participate in the scrum on a rotational basis, the nearest three players form the scrum so that all players experience play from all positions and therefore gain a fuller understanding of the flow of the game. Teach ALL skills to ALL players.

Safety factors must be emphasized at the earliest stage; shoulders must be above hips; the head and neck must be held straight; a wide foot base must be adopted for stability and strength. Players do not push in the New Image Scrum and so there should be little force exerted.

The hooker should be taught how to strike a static ball placed on the ground before progressing to the striking of a moving ball, propelled by a player acting as scrum half. The scrum half should be taught how to put the ball into the scrum.

Key factors for the scrum half putting the ball into the scrum are:
• Feet must be well apart for balance
• Hold the ball near to ends (points)
• The wide part of ball should 'fit' the hooker's foot
• Hold the ball close to shins
• Put in in one continuous action
• Work closely on timing with the hooker.

The ball is put into the scrum, correctly observing the relevant points of law, and the ball is then struck by the hooker and quickly into play via the scrum half. Players who are involved in the scrum break up quickly to become active in handling and support play.

The concept of the scrum is therefore introduced but the emphasis is upon a five second concentration of effort followed by all players being involved in the continuity of play and in particular handling skills. This approach is consistent with the coaching model suggested by Pierre Villepreux.

Binding positions

Top: Foot positions for the scrum put in. The prop's inside foot is back and the hooker strikes the ball with the instep of his right foot.
Bottom: Line out catching

The Line Out

The line out in New Image Rugby, like the scrum, is unopposed in that the team who throw in the ball (i.e. the team not responsible for the ball going out of play) have possession guaranteed. The opposition cannot contest possession; the thrower throws in the ball, two hands from between the legs for beginners, and the catcher must catch the ball with two hands above the head and with the feet off the ground.

The catcher passes the ball to the scrum half who then initiates play with a pass to the outfield players. The nearest three players participate in the line out on a rotational basis, one as a thrower and two in the line out as potential jumpers/catchers.

Catching the ball above the head, with feet off the ground, is a fairly complex skill for youngsters to acquire and so significant amounts of time must be spent practising these skills and those of the scrum. However the tap restart, the scrum and the line out are merely ways of restarting play and all players while they must gain an understanding of play at and from the restart phases, nevertheless must be mainly concerned with play between the set pieces.

Handling Skills

The basic lateral pass has been discussed in some detail. Now a consideration of more advanced handling skills will begin.

Long and short passes

A group of four/five players inter-pass down a narrow (five metre) channel before moving into a wider, return channel (ten metres) where they have to make a longer pass.

Use two ten-metre channels where players make long and short passes adapting to the running and support lines of the other players. Communication is important.

Key factors for longer passes
• Emphasize the swing of the arms - follow-through
• Use arms, fingers and wrists to put more pace on the ball

• Pass directly to the target to avoid lobbing the ball (guarding against interception).

Switch pass

Often used when the outside player who is close to the touchline/sideline decides to come inside a ball carrier to keep the ball 'alive' and in play. This pass can also be used to switch the direction of play in midfield. Teach the pass in a five-metre grid in pairs.

Key factors
• The ball carrier turns to show ball to the receiver (shielding ball from opposition with his body)
• Receiver cuts in close to the ball carrier from behind
• Receiver takes the ball from the carrier's hands initially; developing into a short 'pop' pass.

   Practise switch in both directions before moving on to two versus one practice in a seven-metre grid. The defender allows himself to be fixed by the ball carrier and the receiver goes free to 'score'.

The switch pass

The loop pass

   Gradually the defender can become more active, from intercepting to New Image tackling and to stand up 'smother' tackle.

   The attackers meanwhile progress from walk to jog to run. Eventually the ball carrier has the option of dummying the defence if he feels the defender has not been committed/fixed to the ball carrier and consequently the receiver may not go 'free'.

Loop pass

The purpose of the loop pass is to create 'overlap' or 'overload' situations where the attackers outnumber defenders. The initial ball carrier passes to a receiver and then follows the ball to loop around the receiver and create an overlap or, at the very least, more problems for the defence in that further demands are being made on them.

Key factors
• Make a short, flat pass initially so that the passer can get outside the receiver
• The receiver screens the ball from the defence with his body (creating the option of the dummy later on)
• The initial passer goes outside the receiver and runs **straight** on to receive a short pass. **Hold hands out at shoulder height to create a target.**

Teach the skill in a five-metre grid in pairs. Develop through two versus one, three versus one, four versus two, etc practices.

Contact skills

The lateral, switch and loop passes described have involved a limited degree of opposition. **Contact skills** must now be taught where ball carriers and defenders will contest possession in contact situations.

Summary

• Emphasize catching and passing skills.
• Vary the length, speed, direction, flight and trajectory of pass.
• The receiver sets the 'target' with his arms out and hands up.
• Use rugby related small-sided games to develop a variety of handling skill practices.
• Proceed to New Image Rugby, with passes made in any direction initially followed by passing backwards.
• Free pass restarts are appropriate in the earlier stages of New Image Rugby; proceed to tap restarts, then scrum and line out.
• Handling skills involving decision making, lines of running and the timing of passes should follow once basic handling skills have been acquired.
• Coach skills related to recovering possession of a ball which is on the ground.
• Coach the concept of the scrum and line out but emphasize they are restart phases only (five seconds of concentration) in a constantly moving, fluid game.
• Move from unopposed and static opposition to opposed practices and contact skills.

CONTACT SKILLS AND MINI RUGBY

Contact Skills and Mini Rugby

The New Image Rugby strategy in the 'Introducing Rugby' continuum and all aspects of handling skills discussed so far have been appropriate for boys and/or girls. Now that contact skills are to be taught, it is appropriate that boys proceed along the 'Contact Arm' of the 'Introducing Rugby' Continuum (see diagram). Girls should continue to play New Image Rugby, either amongst themselves or together with boys. Some girls may move on to contact rugby and the development of Women's Rugby will be discussed later. Girls have been successfully involved in club Mini Rugby and no rigid directives are necessary, although mixed contact rugby for beginners is unlikely to be thought appropriate for curriculum physical education in schools.

Contact Skills

Contact skills should be taught gradually and progressively. The teaching of contact skills is of critical importance if beginners are not to be put off the game. They MUST be taught sympathetically and correctly.

Many beginners are often understandably nervous about the physical contact side of many games, including Rugby Football. The coach must develop in the players a confidence in contact. He must take into account the physical differences between players and, certainly, early contact work in pairs and groups should be with players of roughly the same physical size. The gradual introduction to the game suggested earlier by way of New Image Rugby has been formulated partly because of significant evidence from Mini Rugby and Junior Rugby (from eight- or nine- to fifteen-a-side) that the game is often dominated by the physically large player whose size and strength rather than skill facilitates this domination.

Confidence in contact comes from gradual progression through a variety of fun-based activities introduced by the coach.

Some ideas for introductory contact skill activities are shown overleaf. Players should become familiar and confident in contact

NON-CONTACT	
Under Seven	**Under Eigh**
• Play games with small numbers	• Play games with small numbers
• Pass anywhere	• Pass backwards
• Two-handed touch	• Two-handed touc
• Free pass re-start	• Free pass re-start
• Opponents 7m away on line parallel to goalline	• Opponents 7m away on line parallel to goal li
• No scrum	• No scrum
• No line out	• No line out
• No hand-off until 13	• Towards end of season move to concept of set piece positions. A players to experience play i both units - forward and back
• Encourage ball being carried in two hands	
• Size 3 ball	
	• Size 3 ball

Introducing Rugby - a coaching continuum for contact rugby
Coaches should select with care the type of game, the rules, the numbers, and the size of pitch for young players. LATE STARTERS SHOULD BE INTRODUCED VIA GENTLE PROGRESSIONS. Be aware

MINI RUGBY			MIDI RUGBY	FULL 15-A-SIDE
Under Nine	Under Ten	UnderEleven	Under Twelve	Under Thirteen upwards
• 9-a-side 3 fwds 6 backs "Confidence in contact" - introduce tackling • 3 man front row passive scrum (Ball must be won by team putting in) • Off side line at scrum (hindmostfoot) is the same for all players not in the scrum, including scrum half • No line-out • No kicking • Free pass re-start at -Kick off -Penalty -Free kick -Ball in touch • Starter cannot run with the ball • Size 3 ball	• 9-a-side 3 fwds 6 backs Confidence in contact • 3 man front row active scrum • 2 man Line-out between 2m and 7m from touch line. Third forward throws in • No restriction after the ball is caught • Off-side line at Line-out 7m from line of touch • No quick throw-in • No kicking • Free pass re-start at -Penalty -Free kick • Starter cannot run with the ball • Opponents 7m away on line parallel to goal line • Size 4 ball	• 9-a-side 3 fwds 6 backs • As for 10 yr olds but now ADD: controlled kicking (i.e. no fly kicking) • Kick off -Tap penalty -Tap free kick - Quick throw in • Opponents 7m away on line parallel to goal line • Starter cannot run with the ball • Size 4 ball	• 12-a-side 5 fwds 7 backs • Laws of the Game where applicable • Scrum 3 front row 2 second row locks binding around the hip. Scrum half restriction remains • Line out 4 man- 5th forward throws in 2m-10m from touch line. Off-side line 10m from line of touch • No hand-off • Pitch size - across pitch 1m from goal line to half-way line • Size 4 ball	• Use the laws of the full 15-a-side game but be flexible on numbers • Hand-off now legal • Size 4, then 5 ball

of size, ability and aptitude.

with the ground, contact pads and bags and other players.

Similarly practices for aspects of contact skills such as tackling, passing out of the tackle, screen pass, ruck and maul should develop gradually from one versus one activities in a small grid to larger group activities in a larger area.

When coaching contact skills it must be recognized that general principles and guidelines should be coached and not rigid formulae. Every tackle and every contact situation is different and to some extent unpredictable, but there are common principles that apply certainly to the role of the ball carrier. When approaching

Introductory contact skill activities: pushing (1), wheelbarrows (2), pulling (3), fireman's lift (4) and 'crab crawl' support (5).

contact with a defender, the ball carrier must adopt a low body position (low is strong and high is weak), a wide foot base (wide is strong and narrow is weak) and must keep the ball away from the tackler/defender.

Use practices which encourage the adoption of a low body position

Body position

Grid and channel activities which involve the adoption of an efficient, low body position should be practised in pairs and then in larger groups. 'Invite' players to move under a horizontal post to encourage a low body position.

Progression

Walk to jog to run. The players should start by giving or handing the ball to one another before moving on to a short, 'pop' pass and then to a longer pass.

Body position relays can also be used. Here are a few examples:

• Player I, with the ball, runs to the five-metre line, turns and runs back in the low position;

• Player I, with the ball, and player II run together to the five-metre line, turn and bind together before running back in the low position;

• Players I, II , with the ball, and III run together to the five-metre line, turn and bind together.

Contact pads are valuable coaching aids. In this practice the ball carrier moves along a line of contact pads

Contact pads are an extremely useful coaching aid. Players develop confidence in contact through progressive use of contact pads. The first thing is to teach the pad holder how to use the pad correctly. Instruct him to:
- Hold the pad in two hands
- Do not wind the pad holders up in the wrists/arms
- 'Give' sympathetically on contact, do not try to resist the opponent/ball carrier too much
- Hold the pad at an appropriate height for the ball carrier
- Keep his body in straight line, do not 'lead' with front knee/leg.

Progression

The pad can be used in one versus one situations leading up to say five versus one eventually. Use a line of pad holders some five metres apart, one behind the other. Use the pads together with a small gap in the middle to teach breaking through the defence and to develop further confidence in contact.

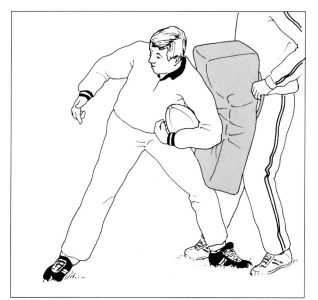

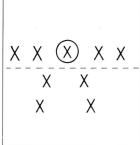

Left: **INCORRECT** The one-armed carry
Above: With support too close/flat, as illustrated above, it is likely to over-run or possibly forward. It is better to come from depth in an arrowhead formation.

Screen Pass

The ball carrier screens the ball with his body from the opponent, in this case the pad carrier. The ball carrier must use the low body position and obtain a wide foot base by placing the leading foot ahead of the pad. If the lead foot is left behind then the ball carrier will face the ground on contact. Hit the pad with the lead shoulder and turn slightly to keep the ball away from the pad. Drive forward in this position. Do not spin away from the pad on contact but rather continue the drive 'through' the pad. Do not turn completely as this will reduce the momentum.

The ball must be held in two hands throughout. Do not carry the ball in one hand and, particularly, do not lead with the ball in the 'front' arm only. When the ball has been presented it can be passed to a supporting player who arrives dynamically at the correct time.

Note
Once the screen pass (one versus one) develops to two versus one then it becomes a maul. The definition of a maul is when at least two versus one players are in contact with the ball held between them in hands.

Screen pass
Promote the concept of 'opposite shoulders'. The opposition is shielded against the opponent by a raised shoulder; if it is his right shoulder the ball receiver should approach him with a raised left shoulder and vice versa. This will have the effect of screening the pass.

Support players should stay deep, time their arrival, be dynamic and run on a line that will take them away or past opponents. If the support player is too close then he is likely to over-run the ball carrier and a forward pass can result.

The screen pass should be practised using both lead shoulders and both sides of the body.

Progression
Again from walk to jog to run, and with increased levels of opposition.

Where the opposition is live, the screen pass will often fail because the tackler prevents the ball being passed. The next player to support the ball carrier will in this instance secure the ball by leading in with the opposite shoulder i.e. if the initial ball carrier led with the left shoulder, the next support player should lead with the right shoulder, secure the ball - four hands on ball-before either passing the ball or moving away with it.

Progression
• Introduce further support players to block/drive/support
• Pass the ball to a support player who moves on to the next pad
• Vary the lines of running - use wider channels
• Vary the maul format - let the ball carrier 'do his own thing' with support players blocking and leaving the ball
• The ball carrier turns; first support player arrives and drives; and the next two support players drive before the ball is played from the maul into a ruck (ball on ground) and the ball emerges ready for subsequent play
• Move from pad opposition to actual, live opposition; starting with 25% opposition and developing to full opposition.

Remember to re-emphasize constantly the key factors and go back to small grids in pairs to correct faults and to teach progression/development. Use conditioned games, say five versus five and six versus six in thirty-metre areas, first with defenders holding pads and then using 'live' opposition.

All contact skill practices so far have emphasized players staying ON THEIR FEET. This is a necessary principle when coaching contact skills; the more players are on their feet then the

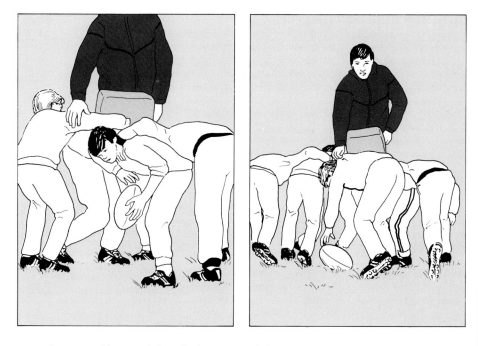

more players are able to participate in the game, and the greater the likelihood of the ball carriers keeping control of the ball and so maintaining continuity. However failures will occur so players must also become confident in contact with the ground.

The ball can be passed - the maul (top left), or put on the ground - the ruck (top right).

Contact Skills on the Ground

Body hardness is an important component of fitness in rugby. Confidence in contact with the ground can be developed through rolling and falling activities, first with and then without the ball. Remember to practise these activities only in wet weather or when there is adequate grass cover.

Activities in five-metre grid

1. Run, make a forward roll in centre of grid (emphasize the need to protect the head and neck by transferring the weight from the hands through to the back and up on to feet again), touch the opposite side line of grid and go down on to the front or side or back. Recover immediately back on to the feet and return to base line. Partner follows. Repeat.

2. Starting on the base line, with ball in the centre of grid, fall on to ball, secure and pick it up and score a try by going to ground at the far side of the grid. Replace ball in centre of grid on return run. Partner follows. Repeat.

Variations

• Repeat 2, rolling ball in grid
• Player I secures a rolling ball by falling on it in centre grid and immediately passes the ball to player II who is in support. Repeat the activity on return journey across the grid with player II making the fall and player I in support.
• In threes - player I goes to ground to secure a moving ball in centre grid; player II adopts a strong, wide foot base position astride the ball and/or player I and passes the ball to support player III. Change roles and repeat across larger grid.
• Speed grid work, putting down the ball and picking up. Start with two balls, and build up to four balls, then eight balls. Reinforce key factors as in Chapter 3.

Tumble Routines

Before coaching tackling it is advisable to coach the concept of 'passing out of the tackle', encouraging players to have confidence in passing the ball to a support player as the ball carrier is on the way to the ground.

Work in a small grid in threes; player I walks (then jogs and runs) across the grid, simulates a tackle by falling to the ground and passes the ball to player II or III on the way down. The pass must be 'on offer' as the ball carrier goes to ground in order to facilitate the pass. The ball must NOT be held in one hand as an immediate pass will be impossible. The ball carrier must know

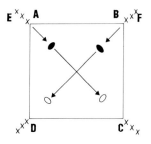

Above: Players in 4 groups at grid corners. A and B start with ball 1-2 metres in front.
Activity: A and B pick ball up on the run, then place it 1-2 metres in front of C and D.
Begin at half pace and progress to top pace.
Start with ball in each corner. Instead of placing ball in opposite corner, roll it towards receiver.
1. A and B go down on ball, get to feet, place ball 1-2 metres in front of C and D.
2. A and B go down on ball, get to feet, turn. Supporting players E and F 'rip' ball off A and B, peel away and place ball 1-2 metres in front of C and D.
3. As above but C and D come to oppose A and B.
4. Introduce more rugby balls

Top right:
Players in unit groups of 2 and 3s for example, tight forwards, inside backs etc.
Activity: Pass ball within groups whilst moving in the grid area. Pass may go in any direction. Do 3 sets of 1-

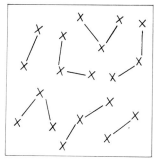

2 minutes. Begin slowly. Final set at top pace. Do stretches between sets.
Extension: Make grid smaller with each set.
1. No dropped passes
2. Avoid contact
3. Utilise space - run into gaps; avoid crowded spaces.
4. Use type of pass according to situation.

Below: The tumble

that support is available on both sides - ARROW HEAD SUPPORT - so that the ball carrier can pass the ball out of the tackle as he goes to ground.

Call this skill 'the tumble'. See illustration below. Move from small grids to larger grids to channels and gradually increase numbers to five/six per group.

When the ball carrier/tumbler goes to ground and support players are not available for the pass because they are late in arriving, the ball carrier must make the ball available to those 'late' players by placing the ball at arms' length. The ball is made available to supporting players and not stuck under or close to the ball carrier's body.

Key factors for tumble routines
1. Ball in two hands
2. Look at the receiver/support player
3. Twist and fall on side, back and rear
4. Pass on the way to the ground
5. Arrow head support
6. Place the ball in static fashion when appropriate.

Hand Ruck

When discussing the development from contact with players on their feet to a maul, the situation whereby a maul becomes a ruck by placing the ball on the ground was outlined. Call this the hand ruck. The ball carrier, turned on contact ,was driven forward by the first support player, with four hands on the ball. The next two support players drove and blocked, and a ruck was created when the ball hit the ground.

Practise one versus one in a small grid to obtain a good, low body position, a wide foot base, shoulders above hips and the ball in two hands ready to be placed on the ground. Build up to three versus one, five versus one then three versus two, five versus three and so on.

Body Ruck

Sometimes it is necessary for the ball carrier to go to the ground to facilitate delivery of the ball. This is called the body ruck. Practise one versus one in a grid, the ball carrier staying on his feet and driving the pad carrier/defender backwards before half twisting, going to ground and laying the ball at arms' length. This is one versus one and there is no ruck at this stage and therefore no offside line.

Build up to three versus one in a larger grid with two support players binding on to the ball carrier before the ball carrier goes to ground and places the ball, ready for a support player and a resumption in continuity. Progress to larger numbers, increased pace and more active levels of opposition.This must be a DYNAMIC, GO FORWARD activity, otherwise it could be construed as collapsing a maul. The DYNAMIC activity will provide good, fast ruck ball.

Foot Ruck

This usually follows a tackle when a 'loose scrum' forms around or over tackled players. Players from both teams quickly gather around the ball in such a situation and attempt to drive forward,

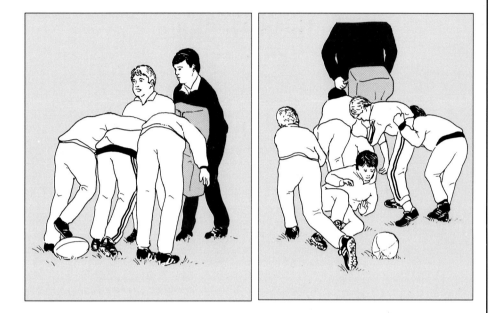

creating a ruck and leaving the ball available for their team.

It is particularly important for the first players who arrive to create a platform for subsequent players to bind and drive on. The first platform may consist of two players (leading to a two-three-two ruck) or three players (leading to three-two-three) but if the ball emerges 'early' when only a few players are involved then so much the better.

Above left: Body ruck
Above right: Hand ruck

EARLY, QUICK LOOSE BALL IS THE KEY TO BREAKING DOWN DEFENCES.

Key factors for the ruck
1. Body position low
2. Shoulders above hips. Look up and forward (not down)
3. Wide foot base - stay on your feet
4. Bind together - take someone in with you
5. Be dynamic, go forward

Tackling Skills

Tackling, like all other contact skills, should be coached sympathetically. Tackling is an important part of the game, given that fifty per cent of the game involves defence.

Correct technique must be coached paying a heavy regard to SAFETY FACTORS. Coach tackling when the weather and ground conditions are suitable. Make tackling activities SAFE and ENJOYABLE and players will soon gain confidence.

Progression
1. Tackling practice should be part of each session. A little and often is the guideline; ten minutes per session rather than an extended period.
2. Ensure that the warm-up practice is related to strengthening and flexibility exercises for the head, neck, shoulder and arms in particular. Use rolling and falling activities too. Remember the tumbling activities described earlier.
3. Work with players of similar size.
4. Begin with players on their knees, without boots. Gradually develop with:
 a) tackler on knees, ball carrier walks
 b) as (a) but ball carrier jogs
 c) as (a) and (b) but tackler crouches
 d) as (a) and (b) but tackler stands
 e) as (a) and (b) but tackler walks
 f) as (a) and (b) but tackler jogs.
5. Begin with side tackle then move on to front tackle and rear tackle.
6. Always ask the ball carrier to carry a ball and present it correctly on contact/tackle.
7. Boots on and gradually develop levels and intensity of opposition
8. Move from one versus one, two versus one to three versus two, four versus two and so on. Then lay small grid games before moving on to channels and then small-sided games. Move gradually from 'token' opposition to the full tackle.

Key factors to side tackle
1. Drive in low, head BEHIND thigh of ball carrier.
2. Drive with the shoulder into the hip region of the ball carrier.

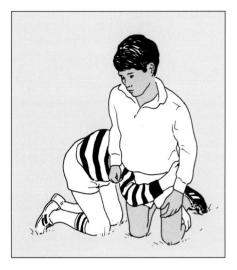

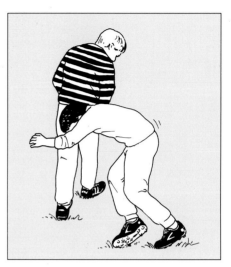

Tackling progressions

Start with all players, both the tackler and ball carrier, on their knees (top left). Progress through phase with both players on their feet (top right) until they are performing a side tackle (left).

3. LOOK ahead, not downwards or backwards.
4. Wrap arms around thighs of ball carrier. Pull tight and HOLD ON until the tackle is complete.
5. GET UP immediately and back into the game.

Front tackle

Similar principles for the side tackle apply to the front but beginners should be discouraged from attempting to drive the ball carrier backwards. Rather the tackler should use the ball carrier's momentum to his advantage to complete the tackle.

Key factors to front tackle
1. Keep head to the side of ball carrier; drive to side of shorts.
2. Wrap arms around thighs, pull tight and hold on.
3. Allow opponent's momentum to complete tackle by falling backwards
4. Turn and hold on to complete tackle
5. GET UP immediately and back into the game.

Progression
Start with tackler crouching and ball carrier walking. Progressions as with previous tackling skills.

Rear tackle

Same basic principles as other tackles.
Key factors to rear tackle
1. Drive low, shoulder into rear of ball carrier's thigh
2. Keep head to one side
3. Wrap arms, pull tight, hold on
4. Arms slide down legs, hold on, stay on top of ball carrier
5. Get up immediately. Rejoin game

Progression
Start with tackler kneeling and ball carrier static. Progressions as with previous tackling skills.

Note
Tackling bags are an excellent aid for building tackling confidence. Some suggestions for their use are illustrated opposite.

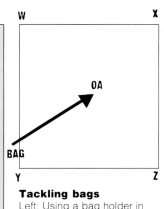

Tackling bags
Left: Using a bag holder in tackling bag practice
Above:Relay tackling using groups of five within the grid. Each group has a person standing at each corner of the grid, W,X,Y,Z. The fifth player is in the middle of the grid with a tackling bag. His job is to pick up the bag after each tackle. W runs out and tackles bag, gets up and runs to tag Z and the process is repeated. Competition: have grids competing against one another, for example, a competition for the first grid to complete 30 tackles. Develop the practice with more bags in the grid, introduce balls or increase numbers.

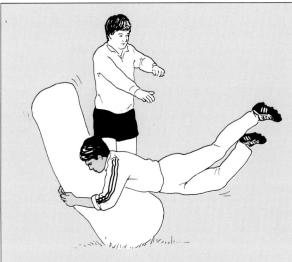

Conditioned Games

Use conditioned games to practise skills coached in this chapter in game related situations.

Play small-sided games so that players are heavily involved and have the opportunity to handle the ball frequently. For example, the attacking team with the ball has to simulate tackle situations and/or tumble routines before scoring. Set the attackers a number of passes to be made before scoring. To begin with the defence offer only token resistance but gradually let a free play situation develop, but always 'load' practices in the early stages in favour of the ball carriers.

Allow each team a stated number of attempts or 'lives' to achieve certain objectives and score a try. The theme for a conditioned game may be a screen pass, passing out of the tackle, maul or ruck technique. Develop one theme at a time and gradually link themes together.

Mini Rugby

The suggested continuum for introducing rugby to beginners has developed from handling skills, through small-sided games and New Image Rugby to contact skills and tackling.

Small-sided games of contact rugby can lead on to Mini Rugby. The numbers per side suggested in the continuum are guidelines only and are FLEXIBLE. Mini Rugby may be played from five-a-side to nine-a-side - Midi Rugby being the transition from ten-to fourteen-a-side. Remember the smaller the side the greater the likelihood of players being involved in handling the ball, which is the prime objective of the coach.

Pitch sizes vary but see illustrations in Chapter 2 for guidelines.

Unopposed set pieces

Mini Rugby should first be played using free pass restarts only to restart play when there has been a mistake or law infringement. The set pieces of scrum, line out, kick off and tap penalties can be introduced gradually.

Initially the scrum should be based upon the New Image Rugby scrum described in Chapter 3. Possession is guaranteed to the side putting in the ball. The three-man scrum introduces the concept of the scrum but the emphasis is clearly upon it being a five second period of concentration designed to get the ball back into play and to initiate handling and supporting play. All players can experience play from all positions.

This philosophy regarding the scrum is to gradually teach concepts of the game to beginners and equally to change the emphasis in senior rugby away from set piece orientation and towards continuity of play as suggested by Pierre Villepreux. The three-man, New Image scrum is recommended as there is little force exerted and safety is assured.

Similarly the line out is taught New Image style. The team throwing in the ball is guaranteed possession. The catcher must catch the ball, two-handed, above the head and play the ball immediately to the half back.

The scrum and line out are unopposed but once the ball is in play then the usual laws of contact rugby apply. Maximize the play between the set pieces; minimize the time spent in scrum and line out phases - players all learn to play between the set pieces. Kick offs and tap penalties can be introduced accordingly but no punting out of the hand or 'fly' kicking of loose balls is allowed.

Total Mini Rugby

Levels of opposition at scrum and line out can gradually be increased until all scrums and line outs are freely contested, always taking into account safety factors, particularly regarding the scrum. Play between the set pieces proceeds as normal.

Guideline laws for Mini Rugby

1. Kick off from centre; '22m' drop out from an appropriate line, say 15m from the defensive try line.
2. No punting or fly kicking
3. Tap penalties at place of infringement
4. Tackling unrestricted but no 'high' tackles. Similarly it may be best to avoid the hand-off technique; note that a ball carrier who has the ball in two hands cannot hand off in any event - NO ONE-ARM BANDITS.
5. Consideration should be given in restricting the defensive scrum- half at scrum and line out. The scrum-half cannot follow the ball around until it has been cleared or he is in possession and runs with the ball.
6. Scoring is conventional except when it is desirable to introduce conversions. The kicks should be taken in front of goal by younger players, then, depending on the age, aptitude and ability of the players, move towards the adult situation of kicking from the line through which the try was scored.
7. The usual laws of off-side, (distances reduced pro-rata on smaller pitches) on-side, knock-on, throw forward etc apply.
8. Playing time can vary between 10, 15 and 20 minutes each way.

REMEMBER, be flexible; adopt a common sense approach and be adaptable. Talk to other coaches about the strengths and weaknesses of players. Help each other.
• Do not let the physically large child dominate proceedings.
• Beginners come to rugby to learn the skills of the game and how to play it so a sympathetic approach is required from the coach.
• When match day comes round, why not play a series of ten-minute periods punctuated by ten-minute coaching sessions.
• There is no time like the present to correct faults that occur during match play.

Summary

• Develop a confidence in contact with all players.
• The coaching of contact skills requires sympathy and understanding.
• Take physical size and individual differences into account.
• SKILL should predominate, not size and strength.
• Introductory contact activities should focus upon fun and enjoyment.
• Develop confidence in contact with the ground, other players, tackle bags and contact pads.
• Key factors are - body position
                     - wide foot base position
                     - ball presentation
• Keep players on their feet whenever possible.
• Tackling skills should emphasize safety factors and be enjoyable.
• Move from grid and channel activities through small-sided games to conditioned games.
• Mini Rugby should emphasize SKILL not physique, and safety should be paramount.
• The ball should be kept in two hands whenever possible.
• Coaches should be flexible, adaptable and should adopt a common-sense approach.

THE SCRUM AND THE LINE OUT

The Scrum and the Line Out

The Philosophy of the Scrum

Restarts

When introducing the scrum to beginners, emphasize the concept that it is a restart phase of the game - a brief respite during periods of vigorous activity involving running and handling skills. Remember the place that set pieces hold in the Villepreux coaching model: not that important.

Attitudes

This philosophy will help produce the correct attitudes in the players of the future; that backs and forwards can have interchangeable skills once the set piece is over.
• All skills to all players
• Greater understanding of the game through playing all positions.

Safety

Warm up thoroughly using flexibility and strengthening exercises specific to the requirements of the scrum. Insist upon a gentle engagement: crouch, touch and engage.

Sound technique: shoulders above the hips, head up, straight back. Wear boots on grass, particularly in wet weather.

For New Image Rugby on artificial surfaces or in sports halls wear training shoes or something similar,

For contact rugby wear mouthguards and shin pads.

Laws

Significant law changes in the scrum for young players have taken place recently. These changes have usually been implemented on safety grounds. They include:

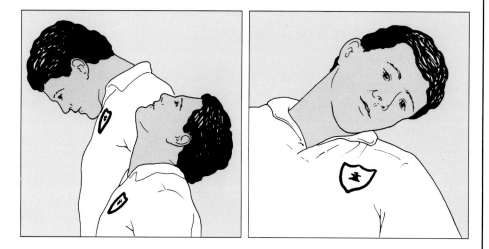

Neck flexibility exercises will help scrum and line out skills.
Above: Flexion and extension will stretch the muscles in the back and the front of the neck.
Right: Lateral extension will extend the muscles on the left and right sides of the neck.

From the UK
• Keep shoulders above the hips
From the Southern Hemisphere where the scrum has been defusd in several ways
• No movement in any direction over one metre (no wheel, no big push)
• No pushover tries
• Defensive scrum half to stay behind his own back feet
• Crouch, touch and gentle engagement.

Observe the laws as directed by your governing body. Adopt commonsense laws applicable to your club/school situation to ensure the safety of your young players.

Remember the scrum is a five-second restart phase of the game.

New Image Rugby Scrum

The New Image Rugby scrum and the unopposed introductory scrum in contact Mini Rugby involve no pushing. Players merely lean on to each other, and there is no pressure exerted on the front three players from the second row. At this stage it is important to emphasize the key factors. These are:

1. Body position - shoulders above hips; look forward; head up; straight back.
2. Bind securely with adjacent players. Aim to get a 'handful of jersey'
3. Props adopt a wide foot base for strength and balance
4. Hooker strikes the ball when put in by the scrum half

All the above are illustrated in Chapter 3.

Progression for contact skills

1. One versus one
(a) On hands and knees
(b) One player locks while one resists
(c) Both players lock and should develop the confidence to put their feet well back
2. Two versus two with the same progressions as one versus one. In the two versus two scrum the players should have their inside foot back and outside foot forward. The players will bind with the inside arm on to their team-mate and the outside arm on to the opposition. The outside arm can be freed easily in the event of a slip or collapse.
3. Three versus three with the same progressions as (1) and (2) above.

In the three versus three scrum, the hooker who is the middle man of the three, binds with both props and has no 'free' arms. The key factors regarding safety assume great importance at this stage. The scrum must be kept as a safe height with shoulders well above the hips.

In one versus one and two versus two situations emphasize key factors without using the ball. When moving on to three versus three scrum, introduce the new factor of the ball being struck by the hooker through the legs of the loose head prop (channel one).

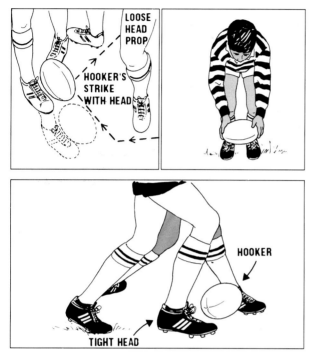

Far left: The hooker's strike in conjunction with the loose head prop
Left: The initial position of the scrum half put-in
Below: 'The strike against the head' by the hooker.

Progression for the use of the ball

1. Place a static ball on the ground in the relevant position, down the centre of the tunnel and roughly at the point where the loose head prop and the hooker meet. The hooker strikes the ball through channel one.

2. In slow motion, the scrum half rolls the ball in to be struck by the hooker. Gradually increase the pace of put in as shown in ilustrations above.

3. Progress from unopposed striking of the ball, through the use of the scrum machine to live but passive opposition.

Strike against the head

Similarly progress as above, except that the ball comes in from the other, right-hand side of the tunnel and is struck with the outside of the right foot by the hooker.

Coaching the Scrum

When coaching beginners it is not anticipated that they will move rapidly towards a full, adult eight-man scrum. The three-man New Image passive scrum has been described, and the next stage in the later stages of Mini Rugby is to retain the three-man scrum but to make it a more active situation while still emphasizing the philosophy of play between the set pieces.

It may be appropriate to move on to five-man scrums when team numbers increase to twelve (five forwards and seven backs). When moving to the five-man scrum the pressure on the front rows is obviously increased. Gradual progressions and continued emphasis upon safety factors are essential.

The same key factors apply as for the three-man scrum. These are:
• The locks (second row) bind firmly together, before going down on one knee and engaging with the front row.
• The five should bind together, crouch and touch before engaging the opposition.
• The second row's bind on the props can be either through their legs to bind on to the top of props' shorts or round the outside of the props' hips, again on to the waistband of their shorts. There are arguments in favour of both methods but at this stage, when coaching beginners, the emphasis must be upon safety and comfort. Coach both methods and monitor which suits your players best.
• The locks' feet should be positioned well back with maximum stud contact with the ground. They should look forward with the shoulders above hips. Point out to the locks that their foot positioning will also affect the channelling of the ball.

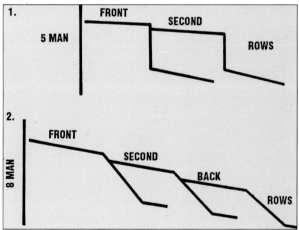

The five-man scrum (above) and a side view (left) of a five-man scrum (1) and eight-man scrum (2)

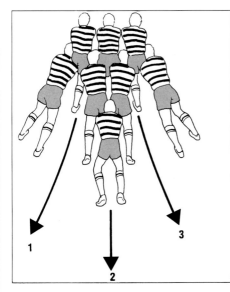

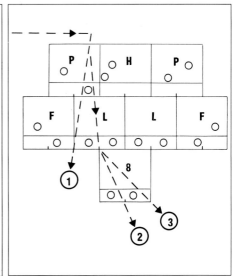

H = Hooker
P = Props
L = Locks
F = Flankers
8 = No.8
O = Orthodox foot positions

Channelling the ball

Channel one (above left) provides a fast heel and quick possession for the backs. All three-man scrums should provide fast heels. When moving on to the five-man scrum, the left-hand lock must take care with his foot positioning. The seven- or eight-man scrum requires even more sophisticaticated foot positioning for channel one to be effective.

Channel two (above right) provides a more controlled ball which the left-hand lock will influence in the five man scrum. The role of the left flanker and number eight in the seven- or eight-man scrum is important too.

Allow players to crawl through the channels to demonstrate and experience them.

Role of opposition (the non putting in team) at the scrum

In senior rugby the opposition ball at the scrum is disrupted by either pushing, wheeling or striking against the head (discussed previously). The wheel is not suitable for beginners for safety reasons and because the use of the 90° law renders this play unproductive.

The drive on the opposition put-in is a co-ordinated push from all members of scrum. The hooker can initiate and co-ordinate this tactic because his opponent is able to put extra pressure on his opposite number just as he is lifting his foot to strike the ball. Instruct the players to bind tight, look forwards, BEND THE LEGS AND DRIVE FORWARD AS THEY STRAIGHTEN THEIR KNEES.

In Mini and Midi Rugby it may be necessary in your role as coach and/or referee to talk to your opposite number and condition this situation when one team is plainly bigger and stronger than the other.

Philosophy of the Line Out

There is no finer sight in top-class rugby than to see a player jump high and make a two-handed catch before setting his backs away on the attack.

The philosophy of the line out, from the passive one in New Image and Mini Rugby to the opposed, contested line out at senior level, is to teach jumping and catching skills to beginners and to developing young players. Coach all skills to all players; you can never be sure that a short, squat ten-year-old is not going to develop into a six foot, six inch international line out forward. The line out is another restart phase of the game requiring five seconds of concentration to produce quality possession with which to re-launch the game.

Coaching the Line Out

1. Start in grids with pairs: one thrower (beginners using a two-handed throw from between the legs, not the torpedo throw) and one catcher. Stand two metres apart to begin with. Throw ball for catcher to jump and catch the ball two-handed, above the head,

Line out spacing

with the feet off the ground. (See Chapter 3).

2. Change the roles and repeat (1) above.

3. Move the pairs further apart until they reach five or six metres.

4. Set up groups of four: one thrower, one jumper, one token opposition, one scrum half. Make them throw, jump, catch, half-turn and feed to the scrum half.

5. Set up groups of sixes, sevens and eights. Use throwers, jumpers, opposition and scrum halves in rotation. Introduce the role of support players.

6. Be flexible when positioning the jumpers. Remember they can stand anywhere, not always at number two, four and six positions in the line out.

7. Passive, unopposed line outs in New Image Rugby and in the early stages of Mini Rugby should produce a success rate in catching the ball. When moving on to active, contested line outs there is likely to be a certain amount of 'bobble' or 'ricochet' ball around. The qualities of alertness, awareness and adaptability are required to tidy up such a ball and produce clean possession for the scrum half.

DO NOT ALLOW tapping from the line out. Coach and encourage catching only.

Key factors of the line out

1. The most important man is the thrower. Coach two-handed, under arm throwing initially leading on to the torpedo throw.

2. Throwers and jumpers work together on timing and co-ordination.

3. Jumpers start from bent leg position and jump upwards and slightly across towards the opposition.

4. Support players move quickly to support catchers or to the area where the ball is in event of a ricochet. All players are potential ball gatherers/ball winners.

5. Constantly vary your line out strategies and positions.

6. Encourage the quick throw in when the ball is readily available. A quick throw is where a thrower quickly passes a ball from the line of touch to a player who has arrived early at the site of the line out before the other players (starts at Under-11).

Line out catching
Left: Four in the line out plus one thrower, jumper and catcher with three alert supporting players.
Below: Individual line out catching

BODY
TWISTING
ON
DESCENT

Summary

• The scrum and line out are merely restart phases of the game that require FIVE SECONDS OF CONCENTRATION.
• Safety factors are important when coaching the scrum.
• Observe the laws of the scrum as adapted for young players
• Quick possession via channel one is the aim.
• Coach the two-handed catch in the line out, with the catch made above the head and the feet off the ground.
• The thrower is the most important player in the line out.
• Progress from the New Image Rugby, unopposed line out to the contested situation in contact Rugby where alertness and awareness are important.
• All players are potential ball winners at the line out.

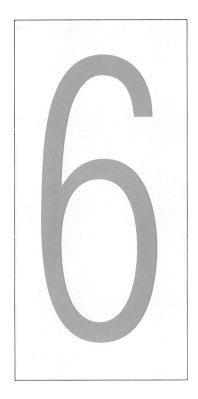

RUNNING AND EVASION SKILLS

Running and Evasion Skills

One of the most attractive sights in Rugby Football is flowing handling and running movement, particularly when a player displays the ability to beat an opponent by side-stepping or by executing a swerve at speed. Some young players may have some natural, innate qualities when it comes to running and evasion skills, but most players will require some teaching and coaching to help them to develop these exciting skills.

In the early stages, when coaching beginners, partner activities with or without the ball can lead to grid activities in small groups. The advent of 'speed grid work' where players are encouraged to move at speed in congested areas, avoiding contact with other players, has been a significant development in the coaching of running and evasion skills to ALL players. (Remember ALL skills to ALL players!)

While natural talent plays a part in running skills, acceleration and agility are, nevertheless, also necessary to improve the evasion skills of individuals. Running with a rugby ball is significantly different from track-running or jogging where the arms have a more important part to play. Therefore coaches must use the ball in most coaching or training situations. The ideal running position in rugby is with a slight forward lean and with the body slightly hunched over the ball. This not only provides good weight distribution for performing associated skills, but also ensures that the muscles are suitably flexed for any tackle that may occur. Running skills require peripheral vision and the ability to make decisions based upon the state of the play going on or around the player concerned.

A correct running position with two hands on the ball

There are four key elements in the coaching of running and evasion skills:
1. Speed
2. Balance (including Body position)
3. Change of pace
4. Change of direction.

Consider the following guidelines:
• The simplest way to make an opponent stop is to run straight at him
• The more you can create a difference in speed between the ball carrier and the defender, the greater will be the advantage to the ball carrier
• Running at a constant speed makes the timing of the tackle relatively simple for the defender
• When changing direction try to get the defender on the 'wrong foot'; slow down for balance as you approach the defender then speed up for clearance as you move away
• Use the feint as you approach the defender by 'showing' him the ball or by leaning in either direction.

A change in direction with a controlled lean

The sidestep

Sidestep

This skill is usually performed very close to the opponent and therefore requires good balance. It is also more commonly used to beat a player on the inside, particularly if he is approaching straight on or at a wide angle. You step in the direction of his approach in this case.

Key factors

These are - the approach, leg drive and getaway, but the crux of the stopping procedure involves:

1. A short step
2. A hard step
3. A fast step.

Approach
1. Sit down with a **short step**
2. Bring the balancing foot up slightly in front of thrusting foot
3. With both knees bent and the balancing foot on the toes, push the thrusting foot out to one side and plant it hard on the ground.

Leg drive
When landing, lean the body back the other way and **drive hard** with the leg, making the next step as fast as you can.

Get-away
This procedure will slow you down so you must now accelerate away, preferably straightening up as much as possible at the earliest opportunity.

Swerve

This is extended much further away from the opponent than the sidestep, up to some six metres. It can be accomplished at comparative speed as it does not involve the same change of pace and direction. The swerve is a great asset to a winger where his main opportunities lie between his opponent and the touchline and this is an ideal skill for the outside break.

The swerve

The key factors are:
Feint
To check the defender you swing the outside leg in towards the defender's inside shoulder. The outside foot actually crosses over the other.

Swing away
Now a second changeover occurs with the inside leg swinging across. This takes you off in an arc as you lean acutely and accelerate away.

The 'Stop'

When you and the tackler are approaching each other at speed you can take yourself off a collision course by stopping dead. The tackler will run past out of your way allowing you time to find support or accelerate away.

Coach these running and evasion skills in pairs in grids, before moving along the 'skills staircase' suggested in Chapter 2.

Other evasion skills involving physical contact are not discussed at this stage because the emphasis in the early stages is to coach youngsters how to beat an opponent without making contact. The hand-off is not coached in the early years chiefly to encourage the ball being carried in two hands.

KICKING SKILLS

Kicking Skills

The Introducing Ruby continuum has suggested that the emphasis in coaching beginners should be on handling skills and small games involving handling. At an appropriate time kicking skills can be introduced. In New Image Rugby kicking should not be introduced until the players are aged fourteen or fifteen, and only then if it is appropriate with a mixed group. In contact rugby it may be appropriate to introduce basic kicking skills at the time of transition from Mini Rugby to Midi Rugby, when the players are aged, say, eleven to twelve.

The danger is that kicking can become aimless and the kicking of the ball becomes an easy option for a ball carrier when faced with an opponent to beat. If a player is not sure what to do with the ball when he receives possession, it is all too easy for that player to kick the ball away.

All variations of kicking skills should therefore be taught to all players. Use partner activities in grids and channels to teach and coach various kicking skills.

Kicking practices
Using two grids get the players to practise kicking the ball accurately to one another, gradually kicking higher.

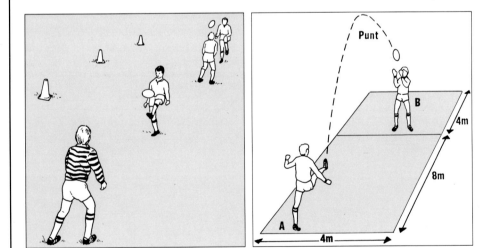

The punt

Coaching Basic Kicking Skills

• Practise kicking skills a little and often
• Concentrate upon one kind of kick at a time
• Always kick to or at a target or target area, let there be no aimless kicking
• Condition small games to emphasize the time and place in which to execute various kicking skills during the game.

1. The punt
Key factors
• To clear the ball to touch when in defence
• To clear the ball when under pressure outside the defensive zone
• To pressurize the opposition through diagonal or high kicking
• To keep the play in the field of play in attack.

Defensive or diagonal punt
Key factors
• Choose the target, and fix the eyes on the ball

Note
The ball must be in the air long enough for your players to be underneath it when it arrives. In American Football the punter has to keep the ball up in the air for eight, nine or ten seconds.

• Hold the ball in two hands, the leading point downwards
• Take a long swing with the kicking leg, make contact with an extended foot and follow through.

Attacking high kick (or Up and Under, or Garryowen or The Bomb)
Key factors
• Hold the ball as in the defensive or diagonal punt
• Lean back, keeping the eye on the ball
• Connect with the ball with the laced part of the boot
• Take a long swing at the ball and follow through.

Cross-kick (to keep the ball in play)
Key factors
• Choose the target and fix the eyes on the ball
• Hold the ball in front of the body and kick the 'wide point' area of it
• Kick up and across with good follow-through.

The chip kick

2. The Chip Kick
This kick is used to get behind the defence and to 'turn' the defence. The ball should be in the air long enough to invite re-collection. The right-footed kicker makes the kick by placing the right hand on top of ball and the left hand underneath it and dropping the ball on to the kicking foot, keeping the eyes on the ball throughout. Judge the velocity of the kick as required.

3. The Grubber Kick
This kick is used to get behind the defence. The kick is made by holding the ball in two hands (at around knee height for a 'low' drop of the ball), dropping the ball inside the non-kicking foot and kicking on or just before the half volley. The body should lean forward, with the head held over ball; eye on ball and push it along the ground with the instep.

4. The Drop Kick

This kick is used to score points (drop goal) and to restart play from the 22-metre line. It is made by holding ball in two hands placed down the ball's sides. The ball should be pointed upwards, sloping slightly backwards towards the kicker and held low at about knee height. Once the target is selected, drop the ball to an area around the non-kicking foot, then coordinate the drop, swing of the leg and contact with the instep as the ball hits the ground on the half volley. Lean over the ball with the eye on ball throughout the shot.

5. The Place Kick

This kick is used to score points and to start and re-start play. Place the ball upright with the seam of the ball lined up with the target/posts. Keep the eyes on the ball throughout the run-up and when the non-kicking foot is alongside ball, use the instep to strike the ball.

The grubber kick

6. Dribbling

This is used to control the ball with the feet in broken play, for example from dribbles from attack that are controlled - a neglected skill which still has relevance to today's game. Control the ball with the instep, keeping the head and eyes in front, over the ball; and using the arms to balance.

It is often appropriate to integrate kicking and catching skills. Make sessions fun for beginners by playing small-sided, ten-minute kicking games.

Emphasize that kicking the ball often loses possession. Make sure that beginners appreciate the value of good, effective kicking but equally that on most occasions it is more productive to keep the ball in the hand.

Note
Most modern day kickers use the 'round the corner' approach and the instep kick.

Summary

Far left: The drop kick
Centre: The place kick
Above: Dribbling

• Effective kicking is a bonus to all Rugby teams - effective kicking keeps possession.
• Avoid aimless kicking and do not allow kicking to become the 'easy option'.
• Coach all kicking skills to all players even though some positions in senior rugby require expert kickers more than other positions.
• Practice kicking during every session; a little and often. Note Dusty Hare practised kicking every day.
• Emphasize that although players need to acquire kicking skills, rugby is a running, handling game and it is usually best to keep the ball in the hand!

THE LAWS AND REFEREEING

The Laws and Refereeing

Many of the laws of rugby will have been introduced to beginners gradually, throughout the Introducing Rugby continuum. The knock on, the forward pass and the requirement to play the ball immediately when tackled will have been learnt in the grid, channel and small game situation. As skills are acquired and an understanding of how to play the game encouraged, then so too will the fundamental laws of the game be grasped.

The Laws of Rugby Football can be a fairly intimidating document to someone who does not have an extensive rugby background. It is not necessary for the coach involved in the coaching of young players and beginners to have detailed knowledge of the law book. However, the guidelines suggested in this chapter will be an aide memoire to the coach/referee.

In the early years of a young player's development, whether in school, club or a community environment, the coach will also be the referee and vice versa. International referees, for example Clive Norling and Roger Quittendon, readily acknowledge that pieces of advice, instruction and information given verbally to players during the course of a game are as vital to the flow of the game, and to the players' understanding of it, as instances when the whistle is blown. The same model is even more valid when we consider young players and beginners. The referee of the small sided, New Image Rugby, Mini or Midi Rugby game is also a coach and he must encourage, correct and advise where appropriate and use the whistle sparingly.

A knowledge of the advantage law and an ability to apply advantage in the game is a priceless quality in a referee at all levels of rugby. Don't whistle for a stoppage when it is possible for the non-offending players to gain an advantage, and for continuity of play to be maintained. The concept of encouraging continuity in coaching also applies to refereeing.

Guidelines for Refereeing Beginners

During 'in game' coaching sessions the referee will be a coach too. Preventive refereeing where the coach/referee gives advice to players on how to avoid infringements is preferable to the whistle being blown, a stoppage in play occurring and a subsequent explanation taking place.

The referee/coach should try to play the ADVANTAGE LAW whenever possible, particularly where beginners are involved. Do not stop play to give an explanation every time there is an infringement. Make some key points quickly at the time, make a mental note of the infringement or fault and make the necessary coaching or corrective points during a natural break in play.

A Concise Guide to the Rugby Laws

Distances quoted relate to the full game of Rugby. Reduce distances pro rata to the size of the pitch when coaching young players.

Kick off

The kick off is used to start each half. To restart play after a successful kick at goal a place kick must be used, and a drop kick for all other restarts.

The kick off must be taken from near the centre of the halfway line and should travel ten metres, unless first touched by an opponent. It must also not go out on the full. If either occurs, the other team may opt to have ball kicked off again or to have a scrum on the halfway line.

Play

The ball goes out of play and a line out is played if the ball is knocked on or thrown forward. A scrummage is played if the ball becomes unplayable.

Play stops if a try is scored (there is then an attempt at a conversion); or if the ball is made 'dead' (causing a drop out or five-metre scrum); a player commits an illegality (penalty); or the ball is 'marked' - the ball-carrier caught by a defender within the defender's 22-metre area (free kick).

Line out

The team that did not carry or kick the ball out throws in the ball. It must be thrown in straight between both teams. Look out for the advantage, but if there is an infringement in the throw in, give a scrum or give the throw to the other team. A quick throw is allowed providing the same ball is used and the ball has not been touched by spectators or ball-boys or girls.

A penalty kick is awarded if there is an infringement of the following:
• Players not involved in the line out (with the exception of the half-back) should remain ten metres back from line out until it ends
• The ball must be allowed to travel five metres before it is touched.

Knock on

This occurs if the ball goes forward from a hand or arm while in the process of being caught, and hits the ground or another player before it is re-gathered. Unless advantage occurs a scrum, opponents put in.

Throw forward

This is a pass that travels forward. Unless advantage occurs a scrum, opponents put in.

Ruck

This is when players bind together with their opponents, with the ball on the ground among them. The ball can only be played with the feet, and players must remain bound on to their own team, until it leaves the ruck. Any infringement and a penalty kick is awarded.

Maul

The maul is like the ruck except the ball is carried. The ball cannot be played with the feet and players must remain bound on to their own team until it leaves the maul. A penalty kick is awarded if there is an infringement.

Tackle

A tackle is when the ball-carrier is held by an opponent and he or the ball contacts the ground. The knee, hand, or shoulder is sufficient 'contact'. Players must immediately release the ball (let it go, pass it, or place it on the ground). Neither tackled player nor the tackler may touch the ball again until they are on their feet.

No player may fall over tackled player or on players lying on the ground with the ball between them. A penalty kick is awarded if there is an infringement.

Scrummage

In a scrummage, three players from each team form a front-row. All binding must be firm and continuous, and no downward pressure may be applied. Any attempt to collapse the scrum must be penalized promptly and severely. Locks must bind around the shorts/hips of the front-row props and around each other. All forwards must remain bound until the ball is clear of the scrum or in the case of an eight-man scrum the back row must step back behind the rear-foot. In New Image Rugby and the early stages of Mini Rugby the scrum-half must stay behind his own scrum and not follow the ball. See the contact arm of the Introducing Rugby continuum.

Penalty kick

Awarded for a major infringement. A direct kick at goal may be taken by either a place kick or a drop kick (three points if successful). The kick may be directly for touch.

Free kick

This is awarded for a minor infringement. A direct kick at goal may not be taken. Any form of kick may be used and may be directly for touch.

Try

A try is awarded if the attacking team is the first to ground the ball in the defenders' in-goal area. Four points are awarded and the team may attempt conversion (place or drop kick) gaining a further two points if successful.

If the ball is grounded first by the defending team, a drop-out (drop kick) on the 22-metre line is awarded, unless the team was responsible for the ball going into the in-goal area. If the defenders were responsible, the attacking team puts the ball into a scrum five metres from the goal-line.

Offside in general play

The player is offside if the ball has been kicked, touched or is being carried by a player of his own team behind him. He must not play the ball or obstruct, approach or remain within ten metres of an opponent waiting for a ball kicked to him by the offside player's team. A penalty kick is awarded if there is an infringement of these laws.

Offside at scrums, rucks and mauls

Any player not bound into the scrum, ruck or maul must remain behind the offside line (a line through the feet of the last bound player of his team) until the ball has left the scrum, ruck or maul. A penalty kick is awarded if there is an infringement of these rules.

Dropped goal

A drop-kick must be taken from any position on the field during general play. Three points if successful.

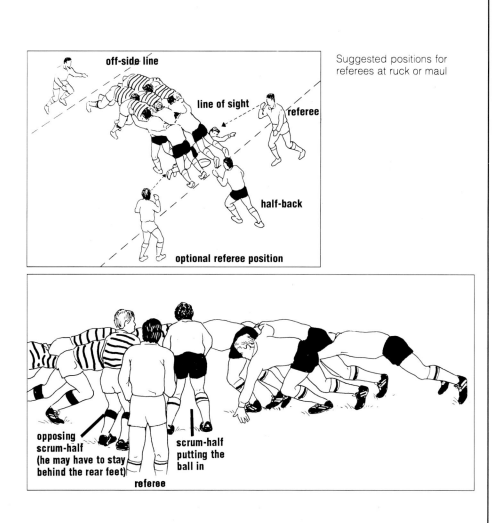

off-side line

line of sight

referee

half-back

optional referee position

Suggested positions for referees at ruck or maul

opposing scrum-half (he may have to stay behind the rear feet)

scrum-half putting the ball in

referee

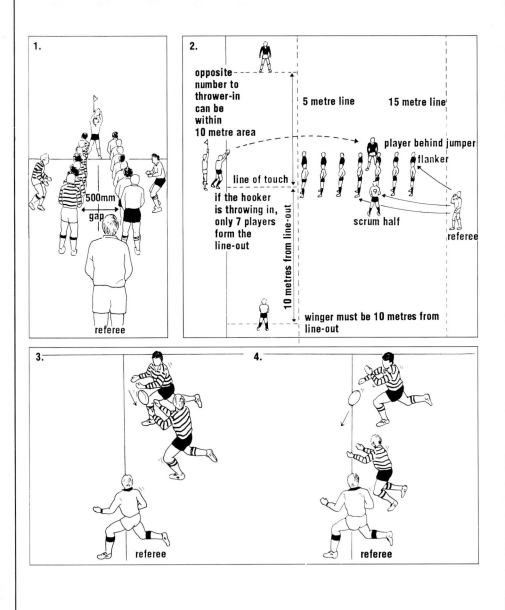

1.

500mm gap

referee

2.

opposite number to thrower-in can be within 10 metre area

5 metre line

15 metre line

player behind jumper

flanker

line of touch

if the hooker is throwing in, only 7 players form the line-out

scrum half

referee

10 metres from line-out

winger must be 10 metres from line-out

3.

referee

4.

referee

The referee's position at a line out

He should stand at the back of the line out to one side (1) and (2) - but he should constantly vary it.

Positional play by the referee

From this position the referee can get a clear view to see if the pass is forward or the player receiving the ball is interfered with (3). This is the best position to spot a knock-on (4). This position (right) is the best to spot off-side from a kick.

A referee blows for a penalty kick to team A even though team A are in possession of the ball. What happened to the ADVANTAGE LAW? Play advantage at every opportunity.

Changes in the teaching of physical education and games, including examinations, profiling, and assessment procedures, have sometimes required pupils to be able to officiate in a game involving a peer group. Given the obvious concern for safety, children should only referee simple games of New Image Rugby under the watchful eye of the coach. Organize refereeing on a rotational basis giving opportunities to all the participants. Involving the pupils in this way helps to ensure that the game is being played in the correct spirit as discussed in Chapter 1.

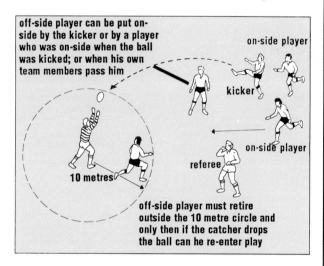

off-side player can be put on-side by the kicker or by a player who was on-side when the ball was kicked; or when his own team members pass him

on-side player

kicker

on-side player

referee

10 metres

off-side player must retire outside the 10 metre circle and only then if the catcher drops the ball can he re-enter play

Summary

• In the refereeing of young players you should be as much of a coach as a referee.
• Apply the advantage law whenever possible and try not to blow the whistle too often.
• Referees should attend coaching courses and coaches should practice the Art of Refereeing.
• Encourage young players to officiate in games involving their own peer group. Obviously close supervision is required.
• Promote pleasant, easy relationships between players, coaches and referees and encourage the immediate and total acceptance by the players of decisions made by the referee.

Further Reading

Corless B., Rugby Union, Crowood Press, 1985

Williams R.,*Rugby for Beginners*, Souvenir Press, 1973

Rutherford D.,*International Rugby*, Heinemann, 1983

James C., *Focus on Rugby*, Stanley Paul, 1983

Corless B.,*Get Ready for Rugby Union*, Crowood Press, 1989

Greenwood J.,*Total Rugby*, A. and C. Black, 1985

Stewart J.J.,*Rugby - A Tactical Appreciation*, Crowood Press, 1986

New Zealand Rugby Football Union, *New Zealand Rugby Skills and Tactics* , Landsdowne Press, 1982

New Zealand Rugby Football Union, New Image Rugby Manual, 1987

Hazeldine, R., *Fitness for Sport*, Crowood Press, 1985

Australian Rugby Football Union, National Rugby Coaching Plan, 1977

Rugby Football Union Publications

Start Rugby - R. F.U. Starter Pack

Even Better Rugby

Improving Backplay

R.F.U. Proficiency Award

Mini Rugby - It's The Real Thing

Mini Rugby - The Cartoon Coaching Book

Mini/Midi Rugby Booklet

New Image Rugby Booklet

Instant Rugby (Laws)

Injury Prevention and 'Take Up' Leaflets (set of four)

Set Coaching Cards

R.F.U. Education Pack

R.F.U. Handbook

Laws of the Game

A Playing Guide

Player Development Directory

Fitness Training for Rugby

Art of Refereeing

Why the Whistle Went

The Art of Assessing (Referees)

R.F.U. Publications Poster

The National Coaching Foundation publications

1. The Coach in Action
2. The Body in Action
3. Safety and Injury
4. Improving Techniques
5. Mind over Matter
6. Planning and Practice
7. Working with Children

Resources - Video tapes

Rugby Football Union

• New Image Rugby (1989)
• Mini/Midi Rugby (1989)
• Even Better Rugby
• A Game for Everyone
• Handling
• Back to the Future
• Running Rugby
• Positional Skills - Backs
• Positional Skills - Forwards
• 101 Best Tries
• Another 101 Best Tries
• England Entertains the 1988 Wallabies
• 1989 Five Nations Championship
• So You Want to be a Referee? and So You Want to be a Better Referee?

Welsh Rugby Union

• Try, Try Again, 3 volumes, John Taylor
• A-Head of the Game (Refereeing), Clive Norling

• Power Play New Zealand, John Taylor (available from retail outlets)
• World Cup Coaching Secrets, Andy Haden (available from retail outlets)

USEFUL ADDRESSES

Rugby Football Union: D.E. Wood, Secretary, Rugby Football Union, Twickenham TW1 1DZ

- London: Polytechnic of East London, Longbridge Road, Dagenham, Essex RM8 2AS

- Midlands: c/o James Gilberts, 5 St Matthew's Street, Rugby , Warwickshire CV21 3

- North: Leeds International Pool, Westgate, Leeds LS1 4PH

- South West: Taunton School, Staplegrove Road, Taunton, Somerset TA2 6AD

Scottish Rugby Union: I.A.L Hogg, C.A., Secretary, Murrayfield, Edinburgh EH12 5PJ

Federation Francoise de Rugby: J.L. Boujon, General Secretary, 7 Cite d'Antin, 75009 Paris

Welsh Rugby Union: D. Evans, Secretary, Cardiff Arms Park, P.O. Box 22, Cardiff CF1 1JL

Irish Rugby Football Union: G.P.Moss, Secretary, 62 Landsdowne Road, Dublin 4

Australian Rugby Football Union: John D. Dedrick, Executive Director, P.O. Box 333, Kingsford, New South Wales 2023, Australia

New Zealand Rugby Football Union: B.R. Usmar, Secretary, Ground Floor, Huddart Parker Building, Post Office Square, P.O. Box 2172, Wellington 1, New Zealand

South African Rugby Board: A. Kellermann, Manager, P.O. Box 99, Newlands 7725, Cape Town, South Africa

National Coaching Foundation, 4 College Close, Beckett Park, Leeds LS6 3QH

Sports Council, 16 Upper Woburn Place, London WC1H OQP

The Sports Council

The Sports Council for Northern Ireland - 0232 661222

The Scottish Sports Council - 031 225 8411

The Sports Council for Wales - 0222 397571

Argentine R.F.U.- Hugo Tucci, U.A.de Rugby, J.A. Pacheco de Melo 2120, COD. POS 116 Capital Beunos, Argentine (840463, TX 22357)

Bahamas R.F.U - M. Lamb, P.O. Box 55 5985 Nassau, New Providence, Bahamas (809 323 2804)

Bahrain - K. Dwyer, P.O. Box 26203, Bahrain. (010973 270328 bus.)

Baillou -1967- R.M.Bease, P.O.Box N4812 Nassau, Bahamas (809-327 7368 home and 809-322 8711 bus.)

Barbados -1957- G. Murrell, Barbados RFC P.O. Box 6W, Worthing, Christchurch, Barbados

Belgium R.F.C.- Daniel Brunet, 13 Rue Timmermanns 1190, Bruxelles, Belgium (02-343-38-31)

Bermuda R.F.U.-1959- M.Moysey, P.O. Box HM1909, Hamilton, Hmcx, Bermuda (809-23 64514 home and 809-29 5515 Ext 1770 Bus.)

Brazil - Luiz E. Gouvea Assoc. Brasileira de Rugby, Rua Prof. Vahia De Abreu 189- Saopaulo-SP-Brazil CEP 04549 (011-282-0563 Home 011-543-2116 Bus.).

Brunel R.F.U.-1977- H.K.M. Smith, Brunel R.F.U. c/o Brunel Shell Petroleum Co., Sendirian Berhad Seria, Negara Brunel, Darussalam.

Canadian R.U.-1929- J. Billingsley, 333 River Road, Ottawa, Ontario K1L 8HP (613-830-0603 home and 613-748 5657 bus.). From 1-12-88 Canadian R.U. 1600 James Naismith Drive, Gloucester, Ontario KB1 5NL

Cayman -1971- P.J. Baxter, P.O. Box 706, Grand Gcayman, British West Indies (809 949 6161 home, 809 949 8121 bus.)

Chile Rugby Federation - Raul De La Puente Pena, Santa Beatriz 191, Provindecia, Santiago, Chile (33314-251215 bus.)

Denmark-Dansk Rugby Union-1950-The Secretary, Dansk R.U., Idraettens Hus. Brondby Station 20, DK-2605, Brondby, Denmark (02-45-55-5 ext.338 bus. 02-544550 Home)

East Africa R.F.U.-1953- J.R.M. Lloyd, R.F.U. of East Africa, P.O. Box 45766, Nairobi, Kenya (528749 home and 336212 bus.)

Fiji R.U.-1913- S.Tuinaceva, P.O.Box 1234, Suva, Fiji (383574 home and 26123 and 24031 bus.)

Hong Kong R.U- 1886-M.J.Haydon, Block A, Room 14001, Watsons Estate, Hong Kong

Indian R.F.U-1971- Mr R.W.Leybourne Callaghan, Indian Rugby Football Union, c/o Consul General of Ireland, Royal Bombay Yacht Club Chambers, Apollo Bunder, Bombay 400 039 India (22202 4607)

Israel R.F.U-Mrs Z. Baran, Israel R.F.U. P.O.Box 6062. Tel: Aviv 61060, Israel. (065 94513 and 94036).

Italy Italiana Rugby Federation - Sandro Di Santo, Federazione Italiana Rugby, Viale Tiziano 70,00100, Rome, Italy (06-691 1537 home and 399485 bus.)

Japan -1977-S. Konno, c/o Sanshin Enterprises Co. Ltd Ichibancho Central Building,22-1 Ichibancho, Chiyoda-KU, Tokyo 102 (Tokyo 7220194 home and 2651561 bus.). Telex 22773 Fax 262-6016)

Kuwait - D.F. McM.Love, Computer Services Dept., K.O.C. Ahmadi, Kuwait (Kuwait 919560 home and 989111 ext.7833)

Malaysian R.U. -Lt.Kol ABU Hassan Ali Hon Sec. General Kesatvan Ragbi, Malaysia, Wisma, Sukan, Majils Sukan, Negara, Malaysia, Tingkat 6, Bangunan MABA, Jalan Hang, Jebat, 50150 Kuala Lumpur, Malaysia

Netherlands Rugby Board - A.P.Steenwinkel, Nederalndse Rugby Bond, Schaepmanlaan 5, 1272 G., J.Huizen, Netherlands (2152 62656)

FURTHER READING

Papua New Guinea - The Secretary, P.N.G. Rugby Union, P.O.Box 704, Port Moresby, Papua New Guinea

Portuguesa Rugby Federation - Marcelino Nunes, Federacao, Portuguesa de Rugby, Rua Sociedade, Farmaceutica, 56-2, 1200 Lisbon (539027)

Republic of China - Chen-Tai Lin, Republic of China R.F.U., 10 Pa Te Road, Section 3, Taipei, Taiwan 105, Republic of China (781 2602, TX. 25714).

Singapore R.U-Anthony Tay Soon Hua, Block 26, Marsiling Drive, 06-223 Singapore 2573 (3682512 home, 2594000 bus.)

Spain-Federacion Espanola De Rugby -1923- Jose Manuel Moreno, c/o Feraz 16-4° Drcha 28008 Madrid (241 4978 or88 home. Telex 47363)

Sri Lanka R.F.U.- D.V.P. Samarsekera, S.L.R.F.U., 28 Longden Place, Colombo 7, Sri Lanka (588011 home, 586834 or 581600 bus.). U.K. Rep. : E. Rajasorriya Manderlea College, 1 Callow Hill, Virginia Water, Surrey

Sweden - Hans Nordgren, Svenska, Rugbyforbundet, Idrottens Hus, 123 87 Farsta, Sweden

Swiss Rugby Federation - Miss E. Obersen, Federation Suisse de Rugby, Case Postale 94, CH1018-Lausanne 18, Switzerland 21234242 Home and 213114 bus.)

Thai Rugby Union-1938- Mr. Suradej, Boonyawatana, Tephasdin Stadium, National Stadium, Rama 1 Road, Bangkok 10500, Thailand (215 3839)

United States R.F.U-1947- Dr. I.Nixon, M.D., U.S.A.R.F.U.National Office, 830 North Tejon, Suite 104B, Colorado Springs, Co 80903 (719-632-1022)

Uruguay Rugby Union- Gustavo Zerbino, Union De Rugby Del Uruguay, Montevideo, Uruguay

U.S.S.R.- P. Etko, Rugby Union of U.S.S.R. 11270 Moscow, Luzhnetskaya NAB8, U.S.S.R. (201 0094)

West Germany - Werner Behring, Deutscher Rugby Verband, Ferdinand Wilhelm Fricke Weg 2A, D300 Hanover 1, West Germany

Yugolslavia-J.Kudric, Sinisa Tartaglia, Balkanska 24, 58000 Split, Yugoslavia

Zambia R.U.-1965-A.Kamilo, Zambia R.F.U., P.O. Box 71324, Ndola, Zambia

Zimbabwe-I.C.L.McVey, President, Z.R.U., P.O. Box 1129, Harare, Zimbabwe (263-10-46007 home, 263-10-706581 bus.)

LAWS OF THE GAME

THE FOLLOWING ARE SELECTED EXTRACTS FROM THE LAWS AS PUBLISHED BY THE INTERNATIONAL RUGBY FOOTBALL BOARD PUBLISHED IN FULL IN *LAWS OF THE GAME* OBTAINABLE FROM THE RFU SHOP, RUGBY FOOTBALL UNION, TWICKENHAM TW1 1DZ

LAW 6. REFEREE AND TOUCH JUDGES.

A. Referee

(1) There shall be a referee for every match. He shall be appointed by or under the authority of the Union or, in case no such authorised referee has been appointed, a referee may be mutually agreed upon between the teams or, failing such agreement, he shall be appointed by the home team.

(2) If the referee is unable to officiate for the whole period of a match a replacement shall be appointed either in such manner as may be directed by the Union, or in the absence of such direction, by the referee or, if he is unable to do so, by the home team.

(3) The referee shall keep the time and the score, and he must in every match apply fairly the Laws of the Game without any variation or omission, except only when the Union has authorised the application of an experimental Law approved by the International Board.

(4) He must not give any instruction or advice to either team prior to the match. During the match he must not consult with anyone except only
(a) either or both touch judges on a point of fact relevant to their functions, or on matters relating to Law 26(3), or
(b) in regard to time.

(5) The referee is the sole judge of fact and of Law. All his decisions are binding on the players. He cannot alter a decision except when given before he observes that a touch judge's flag is raised or before he has received a report related to Law 26(3) from the touch judge.

(6) The referee must carry a whistle and must blow it
(a) to indicate the beginning of the match, half-time, resumption of play after half-time, no-side, a score or a touch-down and
(b) to stop play because of infringement or otherwise as required by the Laws.

If time expires before the ball is put into a scrummage or is thrown in from touch, the referee **must** whistle for half-time or no-side.

(7) During a match no person other than the players, the referee and the touch judges may be within the playing enclosure or the playing area unless with the permission of the referee which shall be given only for a special and temporary purpose. Play may continue during minor injuries with a medically trained person being permitted to come on to the playing area to attend the player or the player going to the touchline. Continuation of play during minor injuries is subject to the referee's permission and to his authority to stop play at any time.

(x) The referee should, when necessary, but not before he indicates his permission, allow baggage attendants, doctors or first aid personnel other than provided in Section (7) to enter the playing enclosure and playing area. He should be strict in refusing permission to persons intending to give advice or instructions to a team, and players should not be allowed to leave the playing area to get advice or instructions. Latitude should, however, be allowed in recognised trial matches.

(8) (a) All players must respect the authority of the referee and they must not dispute his decisions. They must (except in the case of a kick-off) stop playing at once when the referee has blown his whistle.
(b) A player must when so requested whether before or after or during the match, allow the referee to inspect his dress.
(c) A player must not leave the playing enclosure without the referee's permission. If a player retires during a match because of injury or otherwise, he must not resume playing in that match until the referee has given permission.

B. Touch Judges

(1) There shall be two touch judges for every match. Unless touch judges have been appointed by or under the authority of the Union, it shall be the responsibility of each team to provide a touch judge.

(2) A touch judge is under the control of the referee who may instruct him as to his duties and may over-rule any of his decisions. The referee may request that an unsatisfactory touch judge be replaced and he has power to order off and report to the Union a

touch judge who in his opinion is guilty of misconduct.

(3) Each touch judge shall carry a flag (or other suitable object) to signal his decisions.There shall be one touch judge on each side of the ground and he shall remain in touch except when judging a kick at goal.

(4) He must hold up his flag when the ball or a player carrying it has gone into touch and must indicate the place of throw in and which team is entitled to do so. He must also signal to the referee when the ball or a player carrying it has gone into touch-in-goal.

(5) The touch judge shall lower his flag when the ball has been thrown in except on the following occasions when he must keep it raised:-
(a) when the player throwing in the ball puts any part of either foot in the field-of-play,
(b) when the ball has not been thrown in by the team entitled to do so,
(c) when, at a quick throw-in the ball that went into touch is replaced by another or is handled by anyone other than the players.

It is for the referee to decide whether or not the ball has been thrown in from the correct place.

(6) In matches in which a national representative team is playing and in such domestic matches for which a Union gives express permission and where referees recognised by the Union are appointed as touch judges, the touch judge shall report incidents of foul play and misconduct under Law 26(3) to the referee before the match.

A touch judge shall signal such an incident to the referee by raising his flag to a horizontal position pointing directly across the field at a right angle to the touchline. The touch judge must remain in touch and continue to carry out his other functions until the next stoppage in play when the referee shall consult him regarding the incident. The referee may then take whatever action he deems appropriate and any consequent penalties shall be in accordance with Law 26 (3).

(7) When a kick at goal from a try, or penalty kick is being taken both touch judges must assist the referee by signalling the result of the kick. One touch judge shall stand at or behind each of the other goal posts and shall raise his flag if the ball goes over the cross bar.

LAW 7. MODE OF PLAY
A match is started by a kick-off, after which any player who is on-side may at any time
• catch or pick up the ball and run with it,
• pass, throw or knock the ball to another player,
• kick or otherwise propel the ball,
• tackle, push or shoulder an opponent holding the ball,
• fall on the ball,
• take part in scrummage, ruck, maul or line-out,
provided he does so in accordance with these Laws.

LAW 8. ADVANTAGE
The referee shall not whistle for an infringement during play which is followed by an advantage gained by the non-offending team. An advantage must be either territorial or such possession of the ball as constitutes an obvious tactical advantage. A mere opportunity to gain advantage is not sufficient.

LAW 9. BALL OR PLAYER TOUCHING REFEREE
(1) If the ball or a player carrying it touches the referee in the field-of-play, play shall continue unless the referee considers either team has gained advantage in which case he shall order a scrummage. The team which last played the ball shall put it in.
(2) (a) If the ball in a player's possession or a player carrying it touches the referee in that player's In-goal, a touch-down shall be awarded.
(b) If a player carrying the ball in his opponents' In-goal touches the referee before grounding the ball, a try shall be awarded at that place.

LAW 10. KICK-OFF
Kick-off is (a) a place kick taken from the centre of the half-way line by a team which has the right to start the match or by the opposing team on the resumption of play after the half-time interval or by the defending team after a goal has been scored, or (b) a drop kick taken at or from behind the centre of the half-way line by the defending team after an uncovered try.

(1) The ball must be kicked from the correct place and by the correct form of kick; otherwise it shall be kicked off again.

(2) The ball must reach the opponents'

ten metres line, unless first played by an opponent; otherwise it shall be kicked off again, or a scrummage formed at the centre, at the opponents' option. If it reaches the ten metres line and is then blown back, play shall continue.

(3) If the ball pitches directly into touch, touch-in-goal or over or on the dead-ball line, the opposing team may accept the kick, have the ball kicked off again, or have a scrummage formed at the centre.

(4) The **kicker's team** must be behind the ball when kicked; otherwise a scrummage shall be formed at the centre.

(5) The **opposing team** must stand on or behind the ten metres line. If they are in front of that line or if they charge before the ball has been kicked, it shall be kicked off again.

LAW 11. METHOD OF SCORING
Try. A try is scored by first grounding the ball in the opponents' In-goal.

A try shall be awarded if one would probably have been scored but for foul play by the opposing team.

Goal. A goal is scored by kicking the ball over the opponents' cross-bar and between the goal posts from the field-of-play by any place kick or drop kick, except a kick-off, drop-out or free-kick, without touching the ground or any player of the kicker's team.

A goal is scored if the ball has crossed the bar, even though it may have been blown backwards afterwards and whether it has touched the cross-bar or either goal post or not.

A' goal is scored if the ball has crossed the bar notwithstanding a prior offence of the opposing team.

A goal may be awarded if the ball is illegally touched by any player of the opposing team and if the referee considers that a goal would otherwise probably have been scored.

The scoring values are as follows:

A try .... **4 points**
A goal scored after a try ...... **2 points**
A goal from a penalty kick ... **3 points**
A dropped goal otherwise obtained .... **3 points**

LAW 12. TRY AND TOUCH-DOWN
Grounding the ball is the act of the player who
(a) while holding the ball in his hand (or hands) or arm (or arms) brings the ball in contact with the ground, or
(b) while the ball is on the ground either
• Places his hand (or hands) or arm (or arms) on it with downward pressure, or
• falls upon it and the ball is anywhere under the front of his body from waist to neck inclusive.
Picking up the ball from the ground is not grounding it.

A. **Try**
(1) A player who is on-side scores a try when
• he carries the ball into his opponents' In-goal, or
• the ball is in his opponents' In-goal. (and he first grounds it there).
(2) The scoring of a try includes the following cases:-
(a) if a player carries, passes, knocks or kicks the ball into his In-goal and an opponent first grounds it,

(b) if, at a scrummage or ruck, a team is pushed over its goal line and before the ball has emerged it is first grounded in In-goal by an attacking player,
(c) if the momentum of a player, when tackled, carries him into his opponents' In-goal and he first there grounds the ball,
(d) if a player first grounds the ball on his opponents' goal line or if the ball is in contact with the ground and a goal post.
(e) If a tackle occurs in such a position that the tackled player whilst complying with the Law is able to place the ball on or over the goal line.

(3) If a player grounds the ball in his opponents' In-goal and picks it up again, a try is scored where it was first grounded.

(4) A try may be scored by a player who is in touch or in touch-in-goal provided that he is not carrying the ball.

B. **Penalty Try**
A penalty try shall be awarded between the posts if but for foul play by the defending team
• a try would probably have been scored, or
• it would probably have been scored in a more favourable position than that where the ball was grounded.

C. **Touch-Down**
(1) A touch-down occurs when a player first grounds the ball in his In-goal.

(2) After a touch-down play shall be restarted either by a drop-out or a

THE LAWS AND REFEREEING

scrummage, as provided in Law 14.

D. Scrummage after Grounding in Case of Doubt

Where there is doubt as to which team first grounded the ball in In-goal, a scrummage shall be formed five metres from the goal line opposite the place where the ball was grounded. The attacking team shall put in the ball.

LAW 13. KICK AT GOAL AFTER A TRY

(1) After a try has been scored, the scoring team has the right to take a place kick or drop kick at goals on a line through the place where the try was scored.

If the scoring team does not take the kick, play shall be restarted by a drop kick from the centre, unless time has expired.

(2) If a kick is taken:-
(a) it must be taken without undue delay;
(b) any player including the kicker may place the ball;
(c) the **kicker's team**, except the placer, must be behind the ball when kicked;
(d) if the kicker kicks the ball from a placer's hands without the ball being on the ground, the kick is void;
(e) the **opposing team** must be behind the goal line until the kicker begins his run or offers to kick when they may charge or jump with a view to preventing a goal.
(3) Neither the kicker nor a placer shall wilfully do anything which may lead the opposing team to charge prematurely. If either does so, the charge shall not be disallowed.

Penalty:-
• For an infringement by the kicker's team - the kick shall be disallowed.
• For an infringement by the **opposing team** - the charge shall be disallowed. If, however, the kick has been taken successfully, the goal shall stand. If it was unsuccessful, the kicker may take another kick under the original conditions without the charge and may change the type of kick.

LAW 14. IN-GOAL

In-goal is the area bounded by a goal-line, touch-in-goal lines and dead-ball line. It includes the goal lines and goal posts but excludes touch-in-goal lines and dead-ball line.

Touch-in-goal occurs when the ball or player carrying it touches a corner post or a touch-in-goal line or the ground or a person or object on or beyond it. The flag is not part of the corner post.

Five Metres Scrummage

(1) If a player carrying the ball in In-goal is so held that he cannot ground the ball, a scrummage shall be formed five metres from the goal line opposite the place where he was held. The attacking team shall put in the ball.

(2) (a) If a defending player heels, kicks, carries, passes or knocks the ball over his goal line and it there becomes dead except where
• a try is scored, or
• he wilfully knocks or throws the ball from the field-of-play into touch-in-goal or over the dead-ball line, or
(b) if a defending player in In-goal has his kick charged down by an attacking player after

• he carried the ball back from the field-of-play, or
• a defending player put it into In-goal and the ball is then touched down or goes into touch-in-goal or over the dead ball line, or
(c) if a defending player carrying the ball in the field-of-play is forced into his In-goal and he then touches down, or
(d) if, at a scrummage or ruck, a defending team with the ball in its possession is pushed over its goal line and before the ball has emerged first grounds it in In-goal, a scrummage shall be formed five metres from the goal line opposite the place where the ball or a player carrying it crossed the goal line.

The attacking team shall put in the ball.

Drop-Out

(3) Except where the ball is knocked on or thrown forward in the field of play or in in-goal, if an attacking player kicks, carries or passes the ball and it travels into his opponents in-goal either directly or having touched a defender who does not wilfully attempt to stop, catch, or kick it, and it is there
• grounded by a defending player, or
• goes into touch-in-goal or over the dead-ball-line
a drop-out shall be awarded.

Penalties

(a) A penalty try shall be awarded when by foul play in In-goal the defending team has prevented a try which otherwise would *probably* have been scored.
(b) A try shall be disallowed and a

drop-out awarded, if a try would **probably not** have been gained but for foul play by the attacking team.

(c) For foul play in In-goal while the ball is out of play the penalty kick shall be awarded at the place where play would otherwise have restarted and, in addition, the player shall either be ordered off or cautioned that he will be sent off if he repeats the offence.

(d) For wilfully charging or obstructing in In-goal a player who has just kicked the ball the penalty shall be

• a penalty kick in the field-of-play five metres from the goal-line opposite the place of infringement, or, at the option of the non-offending team,

• a penalty kick where the ball alights as provided under Law 26 (3) Penalty (ii)(b).

(e) For other infringements in In-goal, the penalty shall be the same as for a similar infringement in the field-of-play except that the mark for a penalty kick or free kick shall be in the field-of-play five metres from the goal-line opposite the place of infringement and the place of any scrummage shall be five metres from the goal-line opposite the place of infringement but not within five metres of the touch-line.

LAW 15. DROP-OUT

A drop-out is a drop kick awarded to the defending team.

(1) The drop kick must be taken from anywhere on or behind the twenty-two metres line; otherwise the ball shall be dropped out again.

(2) The ball must cross the twenty-two metres line, otherwise the opposing team may have it dropped out again, or have a scrummage formed at the centre of the twenty-two metres line. If it crosses the twenty-two metres line and is then blown back, play shall continue.

(3) If the ball pitches directly into touch, the opposing team may accept the kick, have the ball dropped out again, or have a scrummage formed at the centre of the twenty-two metres line.

(4) The **kicker's team** must be behind the ball when kicked; otherwise a scrummage shall be formed at the centre of the twenty-two metre line.

(5) The **opposing team** must not charge over the twenty-two metres line; otherwise the ball shall be dropped out again.

LAW 16. FAIR-CATCH (MARK)

(a) A player makes a fair-catch when being stationary with both feet on the ground, in his twenty-two metres area or in his in-goal, he cleanly catches the ball direct from a kick, knock-on or throw-forward by one of his opponents and, at the same time, he exclaims 'Mark!'
A fair catch may be obtained even though the ball on its way touches a goal post or crossbar and can be made in In-goal.
(b) A free kick is awarded for a fair-catch.

(1) The kick must be taken by the player making the fair-catch, unless he is injured in so doing. If he is unable to take the kick within one minute a scrummage shall be formed at the mark. His team shall put in the ball.

(2) If the mark is in In-goal any resultant scrummage shall be five metres from the goal line on a line through the mark.

LAW 17. KNOCK-ON OR THROW-FORWARD

A knock-on occurs when the ball travels forward towards the direction of the opponents' dead-ball line after:-
• *a player loses possession of it, or*
• *a player propels or strikes it with his hand or arm, or*
• *it strikes a player's hand or arm*
A throw -forward occurs when a player carrying the ball throws or passes it in the direction of his opponents' dead-ball line. A throw-in from touch is not a throw-forward. If the ball is not thrown or passed forward but it bounces forward after hitting a player or the ground, it is not a throw-forward.

(1) The knock-on or throw forward must not be **intentional.**
Penalty:- Penalty kick at the place of infringement or in accord with Law 14, Penalty (e).

(2) If the knock-on or throw-forward is **unintentional**, a scrummage shall be formed either at the place of infringement, or,if it occurs at a line-out, fifteen metres from the touch line along the line-of-touch unless:-
• a fair catch has been allowed, or
• the ball is knocked on by a player who is in the act of charging down the kick of an opponent but is not attempting to catch the ball, or
• the ball is knocked on one or more

times by a player who is in the act of catching or picking it up or losing possession of it and is recovered by that player before it has touched the ground or another player.

LAW 18. TACKLE, LYING WITH, ON OR NEAR THE BALL

A tackle occurs when a player carrying the ball in the field-of-play is held by one or more opponents so that while he is so held he is brought to the ground or the ball comes into contact with the ground. If the ball carrier is on one knee, or both knees, or is sitting on the ground, or is on top of another player who is on the ground, the ball carrier is deemed to have been brought to the ground.

(1)
(a) A tackled player **must immediately** pass the ball
or
release the ball
and
get up or move away from the ball.
(b) A player who goes to the ground and gathers the ball or with the ball in his possession but who is not tackled **must immediately** get up on his feet with the ball
or
pass the ball
or
release the ball and get up or move away from the ball.
(c) Any other player must be on his feet before he can play.

(2) It is illegal for any player:
(a) to prevent a tackled player from passing or releasing the ball, or getting up or moving away after he

has passed or released it,
(b) to pull the ball from a tackled player's possession or attempt to pick up the ball before the tackled player has released it,
(c) while lying on the ground after a tackle to play or interfere with the ball in any way or to tackle or attempt to tackle an opponent carrying the ball,
(d) to wilfully fall on or over a player lying on the ground with the ball in his possession,
(e) to wilfully fall on or over players lying on the ground with the ball between them, or in close proximity, or,
(f) while lying on the ground in close proximity to the ball to prevent an opponent from gaining possession of it.

(3) A player must not fall on or over the ball emerging from a scrummage or ruck.
Penalty: Penalty kick at the place of infringement.

(4) A try may be scored if the momentum of a player carries him into his opponent's In-goal even though he is tackled.

LAW 19. LYING WITH, ON OR NEAR THE BALL
'The requirements of this Law are now incorporated into Law 18'.

LAW 20. SCRUMMAGE
A scrummage, which can take place only in the field-of-play, is formed by players from each team closing up in readiness to allow the ball to be put on the ground between them but is not formed within five metres of the touchline. If the ball in a scrummage

is on or over the goal line the scrummage is ended.

The middle player in each front row is the hooker, and the players on either side of him are the props.
The middle line means an imaginary line on the ground directly beneath the line formed by the junction of the shoulders of the two front rows.

Forming a Scrummage
P. (1) A team must not wilfully delay the forming of a scrummage.

F.K. (2) Every scrummage shall be formed at the place of infringement or as near thereto as is practicable within the field-of-play. It must be stationary with the middle line parallel to the goal lines until the ball has been put in.
Before commencing engagement each front row must be in a crouched position with heads and shoulders no lower than their hips and so that they are no more than one arm's length from their opponents' shoulders.
In the interest of safety each front row should touch on the upper arms and then pause prior to engagement in the sequence: crouch-touch-pause-engage.

P. (3) It is dangerous play for a front row to form down some distance from its opponents and rush against them.

F.K. (4) A minimum of five players from each team shall be required to form a scrummage. While the scrummage is in progress a minimum of five players shall remain bound on the scrummage until it ends. Each front row shall have three players in it

at all times. The head of a player in the front row shall not be next to the head of a player of the same team.

(5) (a) While a scrummage is forming, **F.K.•** the shoulders of each player in the front row must not be lower than his hips,
• all players in each front row must adopt a normal stance,
• both feet must be on the ground and not crossed,
• the hookers must be in a hooking position,
• a hooker's foot must not be in front of the forward feet of his props.
(b) While the scrummage is taking place, players in each front row must have their weight firmly on at least one foot and be in a position for an effective forward shove and the shoulders of each player must not be lower than his hips.
(c) When five players of a team form the scrummage the two players in the second row must remain bound to each other until the scrummage ends.

Binding of Players

P. (6)(a) The players of each front row shall bind firmly and continuously while the scrummage is forming, while the ball is being put in and while it is in the scrummage.
P. (b) The hooker may bind either over or under the arms of his props but, in either case, he must bind firmly around their bodies at or below the level of the armpits. The props must bind the hooker similarly. The hooker must not be supported so that he is not carrying any weight on either foot.
P. (c) The outside (loose head) prop **must** either (i) bind his opposing

(tight head) prop with his left arm inside the right arm of his opponent, or (ii) place his left hand or forearm on his left thigh. The tight-headed prop **must** bind with his right arm outside the left upper arm of his opposing loose-head prop. He may grip the jersey of his opposing loose-head prop with his right hand but only to keep himself and the scrummage steady and he must not exert a downward pull.
F.K. (d) All players in a scrummage, other than those in a front row, must bind with at least one arm and hand around the body of another player of the same team.
F.K. (e) No outside player other than a prop may hold an opponent with his outer arm.

Putting the Ball into the Scrummage

(7) When an infringement occurs the team not responsible shall put in the ball. In all other circumstances, unless otherwise provided, the ball shall be put in by the team which was moving forward prior to the stoppage or, if neither team was moving forward, by the attacking team.

F.K. (8) The ball shall be put in without delay as soon as the two front rows have closed together. A team must put in the ball when ordered to do so and on the side first chosen.

F.K. (9) The player putting in the ball shall
(a) stand **one** metre from the scrummage and midway between the two front rows;
(b) hold the ball with both hands midway between the two front rows at

a level midway between his knee and ankle;
(c) from that position put in the ball
• without any delay or without feint or backward movement i.e. with a single forward movement, and
• at a quick speed straight along the middle line so that it first touches the ground immediately beyond the width of the nearer prop's shoulders.

(10) Play in the scrummage begins when the ball leaves the hands of the player putting it in.

(11) If the ball is put in and it comes out at either end of the tunnel, it shall be put in again, unless a free kick or penalty kick has been awarded.
If the ball comes out otherwise than at either end of the tunnel and if a penalty kick has not been awarded play shall proceed.

Restrictions on Front Row Players

F.K. (12) All front row players must place their feet so as to allow a clear tunnel. A player must not prevent the ball being put into the scrummage, or from touching the ground at the required place.

F.K. (13) No front row player may raise or advance a foot until the ball has touched the ground.

(14) When the ball has touched the ground, any foot of any player in either front row may be used in an attempt to gain possession of the ball subject to the following:-
players in the front rows must not **at any time** during the scrummage:-
P. (a) raise both feet off the ground at

THE LAWS AND REFEREEING

the same time, or

P. (b) wilfully adopt any position or wilfully take any action, by twisting or lowering the body or by pulling on the opponent's dress, which is likely to cause the scrummage to collapse, or

F.K. (c) wilfully kick the ball out of the tunnel in the direction from which it is put in.

Restrictions on Players

F.K. (15) Any player who is not in either front row must not play the ball while it is in the tunnel.

(16) A player must not:-

F.K. (a) return the ball into the scrummage, or

P. (b) handle the ball in the scrummage except in the act of obtaining a 'push over' try or touch-down, or

P. (c) pick up the ball in the scrummage by hand or legs, or

P. (d) wilfully collapse the scrummage, or

P. (e) wilfully fall or kneel in the scrummage.

P. (f) attempt to gain possession of the ball in the scrummage with any part of the body except the foot or lower leg.

F.K. (17) The player putting in the ball and his immediate opponent must not kick the ball while it is in the scrummage.

(18) A scrummage must not be wheeled beyond a position where the middle line becomes parallel to the touchline. The scrummage will be reformed at the original mark, the ball to be put in by the same team.

Penalty: (a) For an infringement of paragraphs (2), (4), (5), (6) (d) (e), (8), (9), (12), (13), (15), (16)(a), and (17) a free kick at the place of infringement.

(b) For an infringement of paragraphs (1), (3), (6) (a)(b)(c),(14)(a)(b), and (16)(b)(c)(d)(e)(f) a penalty kick at the place of infringement.

For Off-side at Scrummage see Law 24B.

LAW 21. RUCK

A ruck, which can take place only in the field-of-play, is formed when the ball is on the ground and one or more players from each team are on their feet and in physical contact, closing around the ball between them. If the ball in a ruck is on or over the goal line the ruck is ended.

(1) A player joining a ruck must have his head and shoulders no lower than his hips. He must bind with at least one arm around the body of a player of his team in the ruck.
Penalty:- Free kick at the pace of infringement.

(2) A player must not:-
(a) return the ball into the ruck, or
Penalty:-Free kick at the place of infringement.
(b) handle the ball in the ruck except in the act of securing a try or touch-down, or
(c) pick up the ball in the ruck by hand or legs, or
(d) wilfully collapse the ruck, or
(e) jump on top of other players in the ruck, or
(f) wilfully fall or knee in the ruck, or
(g) while lying on the ground interfere in any way with the ball in or emerging from the ruck. He must do his best to roll away from it.

Penalty:-Penalty kick at the place of infringement.

For Off-side at Ruck see Law 24C.

LAW 22. MAUL

A maul, which can take place only in the field-of-play, is formed by one or more players from each team on their feet and physical contact closing round a player who is carrying the ball.

A maul ends when the ball is on the ground or the ball or a player carrying it emerges from the maul or when a scrummage is ordered. If the ball in a maul is on or over the goal line the maul is ended.

(1) A player joining a maul must have his head and shoulders no lower than his hips.
Penalty:-Freekick at the place of infringement.

(2) A player is not in physical contact unless he is caught in or bound to the maul and not merely alongside it.

(3) A player must not:-
(a) jump on top of players in a maul
(b) wilfully collapse a maul
(c) attempt to drag another player out of a maul.
Penalty:- Penalty kick at the place of infringement.

(4) When the ball in a maul becomes unplayable a scrummage shall be ordered and the team which was moving forward immediately prior to the stoppage shall put in the ball, or if neither team was moving forward, the attacking team shall put it in.

For Off-side at Maul see Law 24C.

LAW 23. TOUCH AND LINE-OUT

A. Touch

(1) The ball is in touch
- when it is not being carried by a player and it touches a touch line or the ground or a person or object on or beyond it, or
- when it is carried by a player and it or the player carrying it touches a touch line or the ground beyond it.

(2) If the ball is not in touch and has not crossed the plane of the touchline, a player who is in touch may kick the ball or propel it with his hand but not hold it.

B. Line-out

The line-of-touch is an imaginary line in the field-of play at right angles to the touch line through the place where the ball is to be thrown in.

Formation of Line-out

F.K. (1) A line-out is formed by at least two players from each team lining up in single lines parallel to the line-of-touch in readiness for the ball to be thrown in between them. The team throwing in the ball shall determine the maximum number of players from either team who so line up. Such players are those 'in the line-out', unless excluded below.

F.K. (2) Until the ball is thrown in each player in the line out must stand at least one metre from the next player of his team in the line-out and avoid physical contact with any other player.

F.K. (3) The line-out stretches from five metres from the touch line from which the ball is being thrown into a position fifteen metres from that touch line.

F.K. (4) Any player of either team who is further than fifteen metres from the touch line when the line-out begins is not in the line-out.

(5) A clear space of 500 millimetres must be left between the two lines of players.

Throwing in the ball

(6) When the ball is in touch the place at which it must be thrown in is as follows:-
- when the ball goes into touch from a penalty kick, free kick, or from a kick within twenty-two metres of the kickers goal line, at the place where it touches or crossed the touch line.
- when the ball pitches directly into touch after having been kicked otherwise than as stated above, opposite the place from which the ball was kicked or at the place where it touched or crossed the touch line if that place be nearer to the kicker's goal line, or
- on all other occasions when the ball is in touch, at the place where it touches or crossed the touch line. In each instance the place is where the ball last crossed the touch line before being in touch.

(7) The ball must be thrown at the line-out by an opponent of the player whom it last touched or by whom it was carried, before being in touch. In the event of doubt as to which team should throw in the ball, the attacking team shall do so.

F.K. (8) The ball must be thrown in without delay and without feint.

(9) A **quick throw in** from touch without waiting for the players to form a line-out is permissible provided the ball that went into touch is used, it has been handled only by the players and it is thrown in correctly.

(10) The ball may be brought into play by a quick throw-in or at a formed line-out. In either event the player must throw in the ball
- at the place indicated, and
- so that it first touches the ground or touches or is touched by a player at least five metres from the touch line along the line-of-touch, and
- while throwing in the ball, he must not put any part of either foot in the field-of-play.

If any of the foregoing is infringed, the opposing team shall have the right, at its option, to throw in the ball or to take a scrummage.

If on the second occasion the ball is not thrown in correctly a scrummage shall be formed and the ball shall be put in by the team which threw it in on the first occasion.

Beginning and End of Line-out

(11) The line-out begins when the ball leaves the hands of the player throwing it in.

(12) The line-out ends when
- a ruck or maul is taking place and all feet of players in the ruck or maul have moved beyond the line-of-touch, or
- a player carrying the ball leaves the line-out, or
- the ball has been passed, knocked back or kicked from the line-out, or
- the ball is thrown beyond a position fifteen metres from the touch line, or
- the ball becomes unplayable.

Peeling Off

'Peeling off' occurs when a player (or players) moves from his position in the line-out for the purpose of catching the ball when it has been passed or knocked back by another of his team in the line-out.

F.K. (13) When the ball is in touch players who approach the line-of-touch must **always** be presumed to do so for the purpose of forming a line-out. Except in a peeling off movement such players must not leave the line-of-touch, or the line-out when formed, until the line-out has ended. A player must not begin to peel off until the ball has left the hands of the player throwing it in. **Exception**:- At a quick throw-in, when a player may come to the line-of-touch and retire from that position without penalty.

F.K. (14) In a peeling off movement a player must move parallel and close to the line-out. He must keep moving until a ruck or maul is formed and he joins it or the line-out ends.

Restrictions on Players in Line-out

(15) **Before** the ball has been thrown in and has touched the ground or has touched or been touched by a player, any player in the line-out must not
P. (a) be off-side, or
P. (b) push, charge, shoulder or bind with or in any way hold another player of **either** team, or
P. (c) use any other player as a support to enable him to jump for the ball, or
F.K. (d) stand within five metres of the touch line or prevent the ball from

being thrown five metres.

(16) **After** the ball has touched the ground or touched or been touched by a player, any player in the line-out must not
(a) be of-side, or
(b) hold, push, shoulder or obstruct an opponent not holding the ball, or
(c) charge an opponent except in an attempt to tackle him or to play the ball.

F.K. (17) Except when jumping for the ball or peeling off, each player in the line-out must remain at least one metre from the next player of his team until the ball has touched or been touched by a player or has touched the ground.

F.K. (18) Except when jumping for the ball or peeling off, a clear space of 500 millimetres must be left between the two lines of players until the ball has touched or has been touched by a player or has touched the ground.

F.K. (19) A player in the line-out may move into the space between the touch line and the five metres mark only when the ball has been thrown beyond him and, if he does so, he must not move towards his goal line before the line-out ends, except in a peeling off movement.

P. (20) Until the line-out ends, no player may move beyond a position fifteen metres from the touch line except as allowed when the ball is thrown beyond that position in accordance with the Exception following Law 24D(1)(d).

Restrictions on Players not in Line-out

(21) Players of either team who are not in the line-out may not advance from behind the line-out and take the ball from the throw-in except only
• a player at a quick throw-in, or
• a player advancing at a long throw-in, or
• a player'participating in the line-out'(as defined in Section D of Law 24) who may run into a gap in the line-out and take the ball provided he does not charge or obstruct any player in the line-out.
Penalty:-
(a) For an infringement of paragraphs (1), (2), (3), (4), (5), (8), (13), (14), (15)(d), (17), (18), or (19), a free kick fifteen metres from the touch line along the line-of-touch.
(b) For an infringement of paragraphs (15)(a)(b)(c),(16), or (20), a penalty kick fifteen metres from the touch line along the line-of- touch.
(c) For an infringement of paragraph (21) a penalty kick on the offending team's offside line (as defined in Law 24D) opposite the place of infringement, but not less than fifteen metres from the touch line.

Place of scrummage:- Any scrummage taken or ordered under this Law or as a result of any infringement in a line-out shall be formed fifteen metres from the touch line along the line-of-touch. *For off-side at Line-out see Law 24D.*

LAW 24. OFF-SIDE

*Off-side means that a player is in a position in which he is out of the game and is liable to penalty.
In general play the player is in an off-*

side position because he is in front of the ball when it has been last played by another player of his team.
In play at scrummage, ruck, maul or line-out the player is off-side because he remains or advances in front of the line or place stated in, or otherwise infringes, the relevant sections of this Law.

A. Off-side in General Play

(1) A player is in an off-side position if the ball has been
• kicked, or
• touched, or
• is being carried by one of his team behind him.

(2) There is no penalty for being in an off-side position unless:-
(a) the player plays the ball or obstructs an opponent, or
(b) he approaches or remains within ten metres of an opponent waiting to play the ball or the place where the ball pitches.
Where no opponent is waiting to play the ball but one arrives as the ball pitches, a player in an off-side position must not obstruct or interfere with him.

Exceptions:-

(i) When an off-side player cannot avoid being touched by the ball or by a player carrying it, he is "accidentally off-side". Play should be allowed to continue unless the infringing team obtains an advantage, in which case a scrummage should be formed at that place.
(ii) A player who receives an unintentional throw-forward is not off-side.
(iii) **If, because of the speed of the game, an off-side player finds himself unavoidably**

within ten metres of an opponent waiting to play the ball or the place where the ball pitches, he shall not be penalised provided he retires without delay and without interfering with the opponent.
Penalty:- Penalty kick at the place of infringement, or, at the option of the non-offending team, a scrummage at the place where the ball was last played by the offending team. If the latter place is In-goal, the penalty kick shall be taken or the scrummage shall be formed five metres from the goal line on a line through the place.

B. Off-side at Scrummage

The term 'off-side line' means a line parallel to the goal lines through the hindmost foot of the player's team in the scrummage.
While a scrummage is forming or is taking place:-
(1) A player is off-side if
(a) he joins it from his opponents' side, or
(b) he not being in the scrummage nor the player of either team who puts the ball in the scrummage
• fails to retire behind the off-side line or to his goal line whichever is the nearer, or
• places either foot in front of the off-side line while the ball is in the scrummage.
A player behind the ball may leave a scrummage provided he retires immediately behind the off-side line. If he wishes to join the scrummage, he must do so behind the ball. He may not play the ball as it emerges between the feet of his front row if he is in front of the off-side line.
Exception:- The restrictions on

leaving the scrummage in front of the off-side line do not apply to a player taking part in 'wheeling' a scrummage providing he immediately plays the ball.
(2) A player is off-side if he, being the player of either team who puts the ball in the scrummage, remains or places either foot in front of the ball while it is in the scrummage.
(3) A player is off-side if he, being the immediate opponent of the player putting in the ball, takes up a position on or moves to the opposite side of the scrummage in front of the off-side line.
Penalty:- Penalty kick at the place of infringement.

C. Off-side at Ruck or Maul.

The term 'off-side' means a line parallel to the goal-lines through the hindmost foot of the player's team in the ruck or maul.

(1) Ruck or Maul otherwise than at line-out.

While a ruck or maul is taking place (including a ruck or maul which continues after a line-out has ended) a player is off-side if he:-
(a) joins it from his opponents' side, or
(b) joins it in front of the ball, or
(c) does not join the ruck or maul but fails to retire behind the off-side line **without delay,** or
(d) unbinds from the ruck or leaves the maul and does not **immediately** either rejoin it behind the ball or retire behind the off-side line, or
(e) advances beyond the off-side line with either foot and does not rejoin the ruck or maul.
Penalty:- Penalty kick at place of infringement.

THE LAWS AND REFEREEING

(2) Ruck or Maul at line-out
The term 'participating in the line-out'
has the same meaning as in Section D
of this Law. A player participating in
the line-out is not obliged to join or
remain in the ruck or maul and if he is
not in the ruck or maul he continues to
participate in the line-out until it has
ended. While a line-out is in progress
and a ruck or maul takes place, a
player is off-side if he:-
(a) joins the ruck or maul from his
opponents side, or
(b) joins it in front of the ball, or
(c) being a player who is participating
in the line-out and is not in the ruck or
maul, does not retire and remain at the
off-side line defined in this Section, or
Penalty:- Penalty kick fifteen metres
from the touch line along the line-of-
touch.
(d) being a player who is not
participating in the line-out, remains or
advances with either foot in front of the
off-side line defined in Section D of
this Law.
Penalty:- Penalty kick on the offending
team's off-side line (as defined in
Section D of this Law) opposite the
place of infringement but not less than
fifteen metres from the touch line.

D. Off-side at Line-out
The term 'participating in the line-out'
refers exclusively to the following
players:-
• those players who are in the line-
out, and
• the player who throws in the ball,
and
• his immediate opponent who may
have the option of throwing in the ball,
and
• one other player of either team who
takes up position to receive the ball if it

is passed or knocked back from the
line-out.
*All other players are **not** participating*
in the line-out. The term 'off-side
line' means a line ten metres behind
the line-of-touch and parallel to the
goal lines or, if the goal line be nearer
than ten metres to the line-of-touch,
the 'off-side line' is the goal line.

Off-side while participating in line-out
(1) A participating player is off-side
if:-
(a) **before** the ball has touched a
player or the ground he wilfully
remains or advances with either foot
in front of the line-of-touch, unless he
advances solely in the act of jumping
for the ball, or
(b) **after** the ball has touched a
player or the ground, if he is not
carrying the ball, he advances with
either foot in front of the ball, unless
he is lawfully tackling or attempting to
tackle an opponent who is
participating in the line-out. Such
tackle or attempt to tackle must,
however, start from his side of the
ball, or
(c) in a peeling off movement he fails
to keep moving close to the line-out
until a ruck or maul is formed and he
joins it or the line-out ends, or
(d) before the line-out ends he moves
beyond a position fifteen metres from
the touch line.
Exception:- Players of the team
throwing in the ball may move beyond
a position of fifteen metres from the
touch line for a long throw-in to them.
They may do so only when the ball
leaves the hand of the player throwing
it in and if they do so their opponents
participating in the line-out may

follow them. If players so move and
the ball is not thrown to or beyond
them they must be penalised for off-
side.
Penalty:- Penalty kick fifteen metres
from the touch line along the line-of-
touch.

(2) The player throwing in the ball and
his immediate opponent must:-
(a) remain within five metres of the
touch line, or
(b) retire to the off-side line, or
(c) join the line-out after the ball has
been thrown in five metres, or
(d) move into position to receive the
ball if it is passed or knocked back
from the line-out provided no other
player is occupying that position at
that line-out.

Off-side while not participating in the line-out
(3) A player who is not participating is
off-side if before the line-out has
ended he advances or remains with
either foot in front of the off-side line.
Exception:- Players of the team
throwing in the ball who are not
participating in the line-out may
advance for a long throw-in to them
beyond the line-out. They may do so
only when the ball leaves the hand of
the player throwing in the ball and, if
they do, their opponents may
advance to meet them. If players so
advance for a long throw-in to them
and the ball is not thrown to them
they must be penalised for off-side.

Players returning to 'on-side' position
(4) A player is not obliged, before
throwing in the ball, to wait until
players of his team have returned to

or behind the line-out but such players are off-side unless they return to an on-side position **without delay.**

Penalty:- Penalty kick on the offending team's off-side line opposite the place of infringement, but not less than fifteen metres from the touch line.

LAW 25. ON-SIDE

On-side means that a player is in the Game and not liable to penalty for off-side.

Player made on-side by action of his team

(1) Any player who is off-side in general play, **including** an off-side player who is within ten metres of an opponent waiting to play the ball or where the ball pitches and is retiring as required, becomes on-side as a result of any of the following actions of his team:-

• when the off-side player has retired behind the player of his team who last kicked, or touched or carried the ball, or

• when one of his team carrying the ball has run in front of him, or

• when one of his team has run in front of him after coming from the place or from behind the place where the ball was kicked.

In order to put the off-side player on-side, this other player must be in the playing area. But he is not debarred from following up in touch or touch-in-goal.

Player made on-side by action of opposing team

(2) Any player who is off-side in general play, **except** an off-side

player within ten metres of an opponent waiting to play the ball or where the ball pitches, becomes on-side as a result of any of the following actions:-

• when an opponent carrying the ball has run five metres, or

• when an opponent kicks or passes the ball, or

• when an opponent **intentionally** touches the ball and does not catch or gather it.

An off-side player within ten metres of an opponent waiting to play the ball or where the ball pitches, **cannot** be put on-side by **any** action of his opponents. Any **other** off-side player in general play is **always** put on-side when an opponent plays the ball.

Player retiring at scrummage, ruck, maul or line-out

(3) A player who is in an off-side position when a scrummage, ruck, maul or line-out is forming or taking place and is retiring as required by Law 24 (Off-side) becomes on-side:-

• when an opponent carrying the ball has run five metres, or

• when an opponent has kicked the ball.

An off-side player in this situation is **not** put on-side when an opponent passes the ball.

LAW 26. FOUL PLAY.

Foul Play is any action by a player which is contrary to the letter and spirit of the Game and includes obstruction, unfair play, misconduct, dangerous play, unsporting behaviour, retaliation and repeated infringements.

Obstruction

(1) It is illegal for any player:-

(a) who is running for the ball to charge or push an opponent running for the ball, except shoulder to shoulder,

(b) who is in an off-side position wilfully to run or stand in front of another player of his team who is carrying the ball, thereby preventing an opponent from reaching the latter player,

(c) who is carrying the ball after it has come out of a scrummage, ruck, maul or line-out, to attempt to force his way through the players of his team in front of him,

(d) who is an outside player in a scrummage or ruck to prevent an opponent from advancing round the scrummage or ruck.

Penalty:- Penalty kick at the place of infringement. A penalty try may be awarded.

Unfair Play, Repeated Infringements

(2) It is illegal for any player:-

(a) deliberately to play unfairly or wilfully infringe any Law of the Game,

(b) wilfully to waste time,

(c) wilfully to knock or throw the ball from the playing area into touch, touch-in-goal or over the dead-ball line,

(d) to infringe repeatedly any Law of the Game.

Penalty:- Penalty kick at place of infringement.

A penalty try may be awarded.

For offences under (2)(c) occurring in In-goal, Law 14 penalty (e) applies.

For offences under (2)(d) a player may be cautioned and, if he repeats the offence must be ordered off.

THE LAWS AND REFEREEING

Misconduct, Dangerous Play
(3) It is illegal for any player:-
(a) to strike an opponent,
(b) wilfully to hack or kick an opponent or trip him with the foot, or to trample on an opponent lying on the ground,
(c) to tackle early, or late or dangerously, including the action known as a 'stiff arm tackle',
(d) who is not running for the ball wilfully to charge or obstruct an opponent who has just kicked the ball,
(e) to hold, push, charge, obstruct or grasp an opponent not holding the ball except in a scrummage, ruck or maul,
(Except in a scrummage or ruck the dragging away of a player lying close to the ball is permitted. Otherwise pulling any part of the clothing of an opponent is holding),
(f) in the front row of a scrummage to form down some distance from the opponents and rush against them,
(g) wilfully to cause a scrummage, ruck or maul to collapse,
(h) while the ball is out of play to molest, obstruct or in any way interfere with an opponent or be guilty of any form of misconduct,
(i) to commit any misconduct on the playing area which is prejudicial to the spirit of good sportsmanship.
Penalty:- A player guilty of misconduct and dangerous play shall either be ordered off or else cautioned that he will be sent off if he repeats the offence. For a similar offence after caution, the player must be sent off. In addition to a caution or ordering off a penalty try or a penalty kick shall be awarded as follows:-
(i) If the offence prevents a try which

would otherwise **probably** have been scored, a penalty try shall be awarded.
(ii) The place for a penalty kick shall be:-
(a) For offences other than under paragraphs (d) and (h), at the place of infringement.
(b) For an infringement of (d) the non-offending team shall have the option of taking the kick at the place of infringement or where the ball alights, and if the ball alights
• **in touch**, the mark is fifteen metres from the touch line on a line parallel to the goal lines through the place where it went into touch, or
• **within fifteen metres from the touch line**, it is fifteen metres from the touch line on a line parallel to the goal lines through the place where it alighted, or
• **in In-goal, touch-in-goal, or over or on the dead-ball line**, it is five metres from the goal line on a line parallel to the touch line through the place where it crossed the goal line or fifteen metres from the touch line whichever is the greater.
When the offence takes place in touch the 'place of infringement' in the optional penalty award is fifteen metres from the touch line opposite to where the offence took place.
If the offence takes place in touch-in-goal, the 'place of infringement' in the optional penalty award is in the field-of-play five metres from the goal-line and fifteen metres from the touch-line.
(c) For an offence under (h), at any place where the ball would next have been brought into play if the offence had not occurred, or, if that place is on or beyond the touch line, fifteen metres from that place, on a line parallel to the goal lines.

(iii) For an infringement in In-goal, a penalty kick is to be awarded as provided for under Law 14 Penalties.
(iv) For an offence under Law 26(3)(h), the penalty kick is to be taken at whichever is the place where play would restart, that is
• at the twenty-two metres line (at any point the non-offending team may select), or
• at the centre of the half-way line, or
• if a scrummage five metres from the goal line would otherwise have been awarded, at the place fifteen metres from the touch line on a line five metres from and parallel to the goal line, whichever is the greater.
(v) For an offence which occurs outside the playing area while the ball is *still in play* and which is not otherwise covered in the foregoing, the penalty kick shall be awarded in the playing area fifteen metres from the touch line and opposite to where the offence took place
(vi) For an offence reported by a Touch-Judge under Law 6B(6) a penalty kick may be awarded where the offence occurred or at the place where play would restart.

Player Ordered Off
A player who is ordered off shall take no further part in the match. When a player is ordered off, the referee shall, as soon as possible after the match, send to the Union or other disciplinary body having jurisdiction over the match a report naming the player and describing the circumstances which necessitated the ordering off. Such report shall be considered by the Union or other disciplinary body having jurisdiction over the match who shall take such

action and inflict such punishment as they see fit.

Under Law 26 when a player is ordered off the playing enclosure or the match is abandoned under Law 26 in a match played under the jurisdiction of the R.F.U. the procedure shall be as follows: The referee shall send his report within 48 hours to:
(a) The Constituent Body to which the player's Club is allocated.
(b) The R.F.U. when two or more players are ordered off together for offences arising from their involvement in the same incident and the Clubs for which they were playing are allocated to separate Constituent Bodies.
(c) The R.F.U. if the Club for whom the player was playing is not allocated to a Constituent Body.
(d) The Union for which the player was playing in International matches. Note: In all the above cases the Referee shall send a copy of his report to his own Referee Society.
(e) The Constituent Body in whose area the match was played if he is not a member of a recognised Referee Society.
The Report will then be dealt with by the R.F.U. under the powers in that behalf contained in Bye-Law 13(g) or by the Constituent Body concerned under the powers delegated to it under the powers contained in Bye-Law 13(c) (see 'Delegation of Powers' in R.F.U. Handbook).
Club secretaries shall report to their Constituent Bodies, within 4 days, the name and address of any player of their Club who has been ordered off the playing

enclosure. This applies irrespective of whether the referee is a member of a Society or not.
In the event of an abandoned match the Referee should:-
(i) identify the individual culprits who alone will be disciplined under Law 26.
(ii) abandon the game under Law 6.
(iii) explain to both Captains the reasons why he is abandoning it.

LAW 27. PENALTY KICK
A penalty kick is a kick awarded to the non-offending team as stated in the Laws. It may be taken by any player of the non-offending team and by any form of kick provided that the kicker, if holding the ball, must propel it out of his hands or, if the ball is on the ground, he must propel it a visible distance from the mark. He may keep his hands on the ball while kicking it.
(1) The non-offending team has the option of taking a scrummage at the mark and shall put in the ball.

(2) When a penalty kick is taken the following shall apply:-
(a) The kick must be taken without undue delay.
(b) The kick must be taken at or behind the mark on a line through the mark and the kicker may place the ball for a place kick. If the place prescribed by the Laws for the award of a penalty kick is within five metres of the opponents' goal line, the mark for the penalty kick or a scrummage taken instead of it shall be five metres from the goal line on a line through that place.
(c) The kicker may kick the ball in any direction and he may play the ball

again, without any restriction, except that if he has indicated to the referee that he intends to attempt a kick at goal or has taken any action indicating such intention he must not kick the ball in any other way. A player kicking for touch may only punt or drop kick the ball. Any indication of intention is irrevocable.
(d) The **kicker's team** except the placer for a place kick must be behind the ball until it has been kicked.
(e) The **opposing** team must run without delay (and continue to do so while the kick is being taken and while the ball is being played by the kicker's team) to or behind a line parallel to the goal lines and ten metres from the mark, or to their own goal line if nearer to the mark. If a kick at goal is taken they must there remain motionless with their hands by their sides until the kick has been taken.
Retiring players will not be penalised if their failure to retire ten metres is due to the rapidity with which the kick has been taken, but they must not stop retiring and enter the game until an opponent carrying the ball has run five metres.
(f) The **opposing team** must not prevent the kick or interfere with the kicker in any way. This applies to actions such as wilfully carrying, throwing or kicking the ball away out of reach of the kicker.
Penalty:-
• For an infringement by the kicker's team - a scrummage at the mark.
• For an infringement by the opposing team - a penalty kick ten metres in front of the mark or five metres from the goal line whichever is the nearer, on a line through the mark. Any

player of the non-offending team may take the kick.

LAW 28. FREE KICK

A free kick is a kick awarded for a fair-catch, or to the non-offending team as stated in the Laws.
A goal shall not be scored by the kicker from a free kick unless the ball has first been played by another player.
For an infringement it may be taken by any player of the non-offending team.
It may be taken by any form of kick provided that the kicker, if holding the ball, must propel it out of his hands or, if the ball is on the ground, he must propel it a visible distance from the mark. He may keep his hand on the ball while kicking it.
(1) The team awarded a free kick has the option of taking a scrummage at the mark and shall put in the ball.

(2) When a kick is taken, it must be taken without undue delay.

(3) The kick must be taken at or behind the mark on a line through the mark and the kicker may place the ball for a place kick.

(4) If the place prescribed by the Laws for the award of a free kick is within five metres of the opponents' goal line, the mark for the free kick, or the scrummage taken instead of it, shall be five metres from the goal line on a line through that place.

(5) The kicker may kick the ball in any direction and he may play the ball again without restriction.

(6) The **kicker's team**, except a placer for a place kick, must be behind the ball until it has been kicked.

(7) The **opposing team** must not wilfully resort to any action which may delay the taking of a free kick. This includes actions such as wilfully carrying, throwing or kicking the ball away out of reach of the kicker.

(8) The **opposing team** must retire without delay to or behind a line parallel to the goal lines and ten metres from the mark or to their own goal line if nearer to the mark, or five metres from their opponents goal line if the mark is in-goal. Having so retired, players of the opposing team may charge with a view to preventing the kick, as soon as the kicker places the ball on the ground, or begins his run or offers to kick. Retiring players will not be penalised if their failure to retire ten metres is due to the rapidity with which the kick has been taken, but they may not stop retiring and enter the game until an opponent carrying the ball has run five metres.

(9) If having charged fairly, players of the opposing team prevent the kick from being taken it is void.

(10) Neither the kicker nor the placer shall wilfully do anything which may lead the opposing team to charge prematurely. If either does so, the charge shall not be disallowed. Penalty:-For an infringement by the kicker's team or for a void kick - a scrummage at the mark and the opposing team shall put in the ball. If the mark is in In-goal, the scrummage shall be awarded five metres from the goal line on a line through the mark.
• For an infringement by the opposing team a free kick ten metres in front of the mark or five metres from the goal-line whichever is nearer, on a line through the mark. Any player of the non-offending team may take the kick

---

THIS BOOK HAS SHOWN THE IMPORTANT AND WIDE-RANGING ROLE OF THE COACH. IT HAS ALSO INDICATED THE KNOWLEDGE REQUIRED TO BE AN EFFECTIVE AND SUCCESSFUL COACH. THE SCOPE OF THIS BOOK CANNOT COVER EVERY TOPIC IN DETAIL, SO IF YOU HAVE DEVELOPED AN INTEREST IN SOME ASPECT OF COACHING SUCH AS MENTAL PREPARATION, FITNESS TRAINING OR THE PREVENTION OF INJURY, THE **NATIONAL COACHING FOUNDATION**, ESTABLISHED TO PROVIDE A SERVICE FOR SPORTS COACHES, RUNS COURSES, PRODUCES STUDY PACKS, BOOKS, VIDEOS AND OTHER RESOURCES ON MANY PERFORMANCE RELATED AREAS PARTICULARLY DESIGNED FOR THE PRACTISING COACH.

CONTACT THE **NATIONAL COACHING FOUNDATION** AT: 4 COLLEGE CLOSE, BECKETT PARK, LEEDS LS6 3QH. TELEPHONE: LEEDS (0532) 74802